BURNHAM NORTON FRIARY
AFTER THE DISSOLUTION

BURNHAM NORTON FRIARY
AFTER THE DISSOLUTION

Sally Francis

THE BOYDELL PRESS

First published 2023
The Boydell Press, Woodbridge

ISBN 978 1 78327 674 5

The Boydell Press is an imprint of Boydell & Brewer Ltd
PO Box 9, Woodbridge, Suffolk IP12 3DF, UK
and of Boydell & Brewer Inc.
668 Mt Hope Avenue, Rochester, NY 14620–2731, USA
website: www.boydellandbrewer.com

A CIP catalogue record for this book is available
from the British Library

Contents

Illustrations

FIGURES

TABLES

Preface and acknowledgements

This book is about a place in my village which I love, which has fascinated me, and been part of my life, for as long as I can remember. As a little girl, I was told by my relatives about the Friary's holy well, a tunnel connecting the site to the nearby parish church, Oliver Cromwell's target-practice bombardment of the ruins from the high ground at Burnham Overy Town, and that my great-grandfather had looked after German soldiers at the POW camp on the site. I went to the primary school opposite the Friary, and my second-cousin grazed his beautiful Jersey cows on the precinct. My grand-mother was a friend of Friary Cottage's previous owner and I have drunk water from the holy well many times.

Over the last few years I became more and more interested in knowing what happened to the site after the Carmelites left. It is here that I must thank Dr Helen Clarke, without whose interest in my research, guiding hand and steady encouragement, my findings and ideas would have remained as just notes. Thank you Helen, from the bottom of my heart, for all your wonderful and generous help.

I am very grateful to the many archivists who supplied the documents essential to this research, and to the following for their varied kinds of assistance: Prof. Mark Bailey; Andrea Beckham; Dr Giorgia Bottinelli and colleagues; Tony Bradstreet; Henry Chamberlain; Father Richard Copsey, O. Carm.; Kevin Crossley-Holland; Giles Emery; Alan Everitt; Jill Francis; Winston Franklin; Stephen Heywood; Dr Nick Holder; Jonathon Hooton; Fania Khan; Amanda Loose; Mark & Flic Lowe; Jonathon Mackman; Phil Mernick; Peter & Tony Minter; Dr Mark Samuel; Holly Smith; Dr Sheila Sweetinburgh; Irit Thorow; Drs Peter & Susanna Wade-Martins; Prof. Tom Williamson; and Dr Mark Winterbottom. I thank the residents of Burnham Norton who allowed access to their properties for surveying; plus those people who loaned me a copy of the Burnham Inclosure Award of 1826, and let me see the POW camp items.

I am very thankful to Dr Victor Morgan for his many useful comments on my manuscript, without which this book would have been the poorer. I also thank Victor for stimulating and fascinating email conversations about the Friary and wider aspects of Norfolk's history, all of which added much extra depth to this study.

Next, I must express much gratitude to the Carmelite Order and to the Norfolk and Norwich Archaeological Society. They both awarded crucial funding towards the cost of publishing this work. Finally I thank my publishers, Boydell & Brewer, for accepting my book proposal and for all their hard work in making this title come to fruition.

Abbreviations

Short-title citations are given in the text. The full references are in the Bibliography.

Add.	additional
BL	British Library
CPR	*Calendar of Patent Rolls*
CRO	Cornwall Record Office (Kresen Kernow)
KILLM	King's Lynn Museums
L&P	*Letters and Papers*
NHER	Norfolk Historic Environment Record
NHLE	National Heritage List for England
MS	manuscript
NMS	Norfolk Museum Services
NRO	Norfolk Record Office
NWHCM	Norwich Castle Museum
ODNB	*Oxford Dictionary of National Biography*
OED	*Oxford English Dictionary*
SRO	Suffolk Record Office
TNA	The National Archives
Valor	*Valor Ecclesiasticus*
VCH Norfolk	*Victoria County History of Norfolk*
WYAS	West Yorkshire Archive Service, Calderdale

1

Burnham Norton Carmelite Friary: context and history

The Order of Carmelites (the Whitefriars) originated as a band of hermits living on Mount Carmel near Haifa in Israel, possibly from as early as the 1160s.[1] Christian forces secured the area by 1192. Within a short time, the hermits appealed to the patriarch of Jerusalem, Albert Avogadro, who provided them with a *formula vitae*, a set of guidelines for them to establish a more formalised community. The Carmelites now lived in silence and poverty, remaining in their separate cells apart from a single daily celebration of mass in their church.[2] They were governed by a prior, a 'first amongst equals'. Between 1226 and 1229, three papal bulls gave approval of their way of life and their community grew. However, increasing attacks by neighbouring Muslim kingdoms made the hermits' position precarious and prompted them to found new sites elsewhere: Cyprus in 1235, then Messina (Sicily) and Les Aygalades (France) by *c.*1238.[3]

Shortly afterwards, Richard of Cornwall led a group of soldiers as part of the Barons' Crusade, arriving in Acre in 1241. Tradition has it that when two of his noblemen visited Mt. Carmel they discovered a fellow Northumbrian, Ralph Fresburn, an ex-crusader who had been living as a hermit there for twenty years. They 'besought the Prior to allow them to take him home with them and found a Carmelite

---

[1] Andrews, *Other Friars*, p.10.
[2] Jacques de Vitry, bishop of Acre 1216–1227, described the hermits, 'in little cells like so many hives where, as bees of the Lord, they produced the honey of spiritual sweetness' (*ibid.*, p.13).
[3] Ribot (trans. and ed. Copsey), *Ten Books*, p.vii.

house in Northumberland' and so a small colony of Carmelites led by Ivo the Breton left for England with the Earl of Cornwall's retinue.[4] Under the patronage of some of Cornwall's knights, the Carmelites, beginning in 1242, built their first houses at Hulne (Northumberland), Aylesford (Kent) and Lossenham (or Losenham, Kent). They also established a house at Bradmer, in Burnham Norton on the north Norfolk coast,[5] founded between 1242 and 1247 by Sir William de Calthorp (probably lord of Burnham Thorpe manor) and Sir Ralph de Hemenhale (holder of part of Polstead Hall, another local manor).[6] Calthorp and Hemenhale were probably also part of Cornwall's forces, which included many unidentified knights.[7] It is likely that two early members of the Burnham Norton house, Peter and Reginald Folsham, had been hermits on Mt. Carmel, rather than being men who later joined the group after it arrived in England.[8] However, their surname suggests a Norfolk connection: Foulsham (Domesday, 'Folsham') being a village *c.*28km (17.6 miles) south-east of Burnham Norton.

Bradmer was a modest hermitage, located, it is thought, near an isolated inlet on the edge of the saltmarshes marked 'Bradmere' on maps (but still pronounced 'Bradmer' by local people).[9] This was

4   Sheppard, *English Carmelites*, pp.4–5.
5   Clarke, 'Hermits to Whitefriars', pp.109–21. By tradition, Hulne and Aylesford were the first two Carmelite houses in England (Sheppard, *English Carmelites*, pp.3–7).
6   *VCH Norfolk*, vol. II, pp.425–6; Francis, *Burnham Norton*, p.9; Alban, 'Benefactors Great and Small', pp.156–7.
7   Clarke, 'Hermits to Whitefriars', p.106.
8   Copsey, 'Burnham Norton: A Chronology', p.234. Three Folshams were described thus: 'Godfrey, Reginald and Peter, all surnamed Folsham, shone in the convent at Burnham, fathers who were worthy of veneration' (*ibid.*, p.226).
9   Although the location of Bradmer is a topic outside the scope of this book on the Friary's post-Dissolution history, some useful notes about Bradmer are added here. As well as 'Bradmere' or 'Bradmore' (which appear on various maps), the local toponym 'Bradmer Hill' is in verbal use for another spot nearby. A messuage with 3 acres near 'Berdemere' was recorded in 1301 (TNA WARD 2/34/132/1). During the 'Imagined Land' project (see footnote 50), there was some local speculation that Bradmere House (TF 82205 44011; nineteenth century in date) in Burnham Norton might be the site of the Carmelites' hermitage, though there is no evidence for or against this being so.

roughly equidistant between the two nearest settlements, Burnhams Deepdale and Norton. Nevertheless, it was situated well away from the thirteenth-century village of Burnham Norton, which was then probably still clustered around the parish church of St Margaret, *c*.2km (1.2 miles) to the south-east (see Fig. 1). No traces of the hermitage have been discovered.

A revision of the Carmelite Rule in 1247 ('the Mitigation') meant that the brethren exchanged their eremitical way of life for one as mendicants, and they relocated in 1253 to a new site *c*.300m (0.19 miles) east of Burnham Norton church.[10] Their new Friary[11] stood on the opposite side of the River Burn to Burnham Overy Town, beside a spring identified as a holy well, and a busy road (now lost).[12] This road may have once represented the lowest, although still tide-dependent, crossing of the valley floor and river. Now, the Carmelites were geographically much closer to the local community and better placed to preach to residents and travellers, and to attract the donation of alms, their main source of income. An additional factor that may have influenced the Carmelites' decision-making was an increase in storminess in the thirteenth century which might have made Bradmer prone to flooding and therefore an unsustainable location for the brethren.[13]

It is noteworthy that the original foundation at Bradmer was beside one of Burnham Norton's commons, then the Carmelites relocated next to the parish's other common. Ironically, the village itself migrated away from the church and the new Friary to its present position near to the sea, close to the probable site of the original hermitage. Although a local tradition persists that the old village was abandoned after the Black Death, its relocation had probably happened by the late thirteenth century.[14]

---

[10] This was the year in which Pope Innocent gave the Carmelites permission to preach and hear confession (Andrews, *Other Friars*, p.17).

[11] Historically often known as Burnham Priory. The Friary was dedicated to the Blessed Virgin Mary.

[12] Called 'Overy and Brancaster Old Road' on the 1825 enclosure map. Its earlier name is discussed on p.31. The late Gillian Beckett first highlighted the importance of this road to the present author, many years ago in a guided walk around the Burnhams.

[13] Hooton, 'Imagined Coastlines', pp.7–8.

[14] Rogerson, 'Burnhams from the Fifth to the Fourteenth Centuries', p.38.

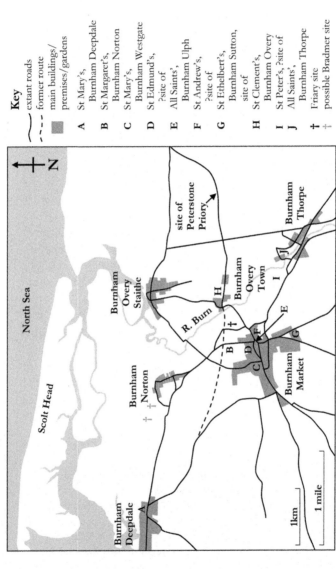

Figure 1. The modern Burnhams, showing possible sites of the Bradmer hermitage, and the location of the Friary. The village of Burnham Norton was originally clustered around its church of St Margaret (B in the figure). Andrew Rogerson (Burnhams from the Fifth to the Fourteenth Centuries', p.42 n.1) argues that St Edmund's was not a separate church building, but was a portion of St Mary's Burnham Westgate, and the name of an area in Burnham for tithe-paying purposes. © The author.

Friaries are normally associated with urban places, but Burnham Norton is a rural backwater today and it seems puzzling that it, and the surrounding villages, could have supported the Carmelites until the Dissolution. However, this is an erroneous perspective skewed by a modern view point. Burnham Norton is one of several villages bearing the Burnham name. These were originally a single territory and a place of much local significance during the Saxon period, when a major 'productive site' occupied a position in the Burn valley close to the old road mentioned above.[15] Domesday describes a populous community ('Brunham'), with a royal manor, mills and salt pans. Peterstone Priory, a house of Augustinian Canons, was founded in Burnham Overy before 1200.[16] A market was established before 1209 which caused the settlement of Burnham Market to develop on land between the churches of Burnhams Westgate and Ulph.[17] Charters were later given for fairs.[18] Excluding the outlying village of Burnham Deepdale to the north-west, the main group had nine parish churches within an area of 2.5km^2 (0.97 square miles) and this is 'unparalleled in a rural context'.[19]

The wealth of the Burnhams was due to their geography: they lie on soil of recognised fertility,[20] and they surround the valley of the River Burn, an excellent natural harbour.[21] When the Friary was built in 1253, the heart of the 'Port of Burnham' was probably at Burnham Overy Town. Here stands the medieval church of St Clement, a

---

[15] Williamson, 'Landscape Context', forthcoming.
[16] *VCH Norfolk*, vol. II, p.391.
[17] Williamson, *Origins of Norfolk*, pp.92–3.
[18] Rogerson, 'Burnhams from the Fifth to the Fourteenth Centuries', p.39. Pevsner & Wilson (*Buildings of England, Norfolk 2*, p.226) consider the thirteenth as 'the great century for the Burnhams'.
[19] Williamson, 'Landscape Context', forthcoming.
[20] Young, *Agriculture of Norfolk*, p.10. Young wrote that all along the coast between Holkham and Hunstanton, '… there is a tract between the marshes and the sand [the higher land], from half a mile to a mile broad, of a singularly fertile loam: it has tenacity sufficient to adhere into clods easily broken, and to produce great crops of vegetables demanding the richest soils; at the same time it has that dryness and friability which renders it excellent turnip land'.
[21] Offshore there was a substantial oyster fishery, which would have added to the area's prosperity. See Smith, 'Beyond the Sea Wall'.

dedication associated with crossing places near riverside wharves.[22] There were also staithes at Burnham Norton,[23] and possibly upstream at Burnham Thorpe.[24] Archival references to the port of Brunham/ Burnham begin in the second half of the thirteenth century and show that, as well as coastal trade, commerce was also conducted with Germany.[25] In the fourteenth century, ships were requested from Burnham for military service.[26] Possible trade links are implied with Gascony or Poitou, and by the early 1500s coal was shipped from Newcastle (in exchange for cereals) with an average of 15 trips being made each year.[27] Calthorp and Hemenhale's provision of an isolated place for a hermitage first brought the Carmelites to the Burnhams. However, it was the ability of these founders (or their descendants) to donate a new site near a flourishing port and river crossing that allowed the Friary to thrive and develop.

After their first Norfolk foundation at Bradmer, the Carmelite Order went on to establish friaries throughout the county, at Norwich (1256), King's Lynn (c.1260), Great Yarmouth (1276) and Blakeney (after 1296).[28] Uniquely, all the Carmelites' Norfolk foundations were at the county's major thirteenth-century ports: Burnham Norton being part of the port of Burnham; Norwich being served by the River Wensum; King's Lynn by the estuary of the Great Ouse; Great Yarmouth, the

---

[22] Jones, *Saints in the Landscape*, p.153.

[23] Francis, *Burnham Norton*, p.28; NRO C/Sca 1/1 mm. 42–42d; NRO WAL 964/1, 284X1; Williamson, 'Landscape Context', forthcoming.

[24] Pevsner & Wilson, *Buildings of England, Norfolk 2*, p.226.

[25] There was an act of piracy in 1265 against a vessel from Rouen passing 'Scardeburg' (?Scarborough) in which the stolen ship and goods were taken to the 'port of Brunham' by men including three Burnham residents (*CPR Hen. III*, vol. V, p.480). Two German merchants complained (in 1293) that when their ship was at the port of Burnham, local people had stolen goods from it (*CPR Edw. I*, vol. III, p.114).

[26] E.g. *CPR Edw. I*, vol. III, p.583.

[27] Hooton, 'Imagined Coastlines', pp.11–12, 14.

[28] *VCH Norfolk*, vol. II, pp.425–33. Blakeney was founded between 1305 and 1316 (Wright, 'Blakeney Carmelite Friary', p.5). The other major Orders of friars were present in Norfolk too: the Augustinians (Austin Friars) and Dominicans (Blackfriars) at Norwich, Lynn, Great Yarmouth and Thetford; the Franciscans (Greyfriars) at Norwich, Lynn, Great Yarmouth and Walsingham (*VCH Norfolk*, vol. II, pp.426–38).

Yare; and Blakeney, the Glaven. Like the Burnhams, Blakeney, together with its neighbours Wiveton and Cley, functioned as a quasi-urban centre for coastal and international commerce. These three Glaven villages and their neighbourhood were evidently prosperous enough to sustain one friary (Blakeney Friary),[29] but it is interesting that this was a Carmelite house and not a religious community of another Order. It may be speculated that because of their locations, the Carmelites might have provided special pastoral care for sailors and merchants.[30]

The Friary would have made a large impact on local life through its brothers' preaching, it being a place of pilgrimage (to the gatehouse chapel, see p.65 and possibly also to the holy well see p.127), and an alternative place of worship to the parish churches. It was the home of a guild, a seat of learning, a place of burial and a small-scale employer.[31] It hosted eight Provincial Chapters, meetings where the representatives from houses all over the English Province assembled to discuss Carmelite matters,[32] and Burnham Norton friars rose to prominence within the Order. The Friary may have contained 15–17 Carmelites and novices according to the terms of a local will of 1505,[33] though this interpretation is not universally accepted and the figure is contentious. It should also be remembered that individual Carmelites travelled between the Order's houses, some of them spending time in Oxford or Cambridge, so numbers may always have fluctuated.

Burnham Norton's Carmelites survived on a combination of alms, rents from their estate (68 acres in 1535; 27.52ha);[34] bequests, as evidenced in several local wills;[35] and their own private incomes in some instances.[36] There is also a chance that one or more corrodians

---

[29] Historically also called Snitterley Friary.
[30] Spindler ('Between Sea and City', p.184) notes that in Bruges, 'Scottish and German merchants were usually based near the Carmelite house, which served as a centre for worship and administration for their respective nations.'
[31] A layman worked at Burnham Norton Friary's guesthouse (Richard Copsey pers. comm., 7 May 2021).
[32] Copsey, 'Burnham Norton: A Chronology', pp.216–21.
[33] NHLE 1013095.
[34] *Valor Ecclesiasticus*, vol. III, p.371.
[35] Alban, 'Benefactors Great and Small', pp.155–74.
[36] There were four known cases (Copsey, 'Burnham Norton: A Chronology', pp.231, 233, 244, 247).

lived at the Friary, as was the case at the Lynn Carmelite house.[37] Burnham Norton's friars maybe also gained an income by controlling the ford of the Burn or providing a ferry there at high water.[38] However, this latter income stream was probably lost well before the Dissolution. In c.1421 the prior of Walsingham built a 'a good bridge, for travellers on the high way from *St Andrew's* to *St Clement's* [Burnham Overy] parish',[39] by-passing the Friary to the south and leading travellers directly into Burnham Market. In addition, sea level change, silting and increasing tonnages of ships meant that maritime activity eventually moved downstream from Burnham Overy Town to Overy Staithe.[40] These two changes left the Friary somewhat marooned. The old road beside it was no longer the busy, main route to the commercial centres of the Burnhams: the marketplace and port.

Political winds of change began blowing in 1534, when all friars were made to sign Henry VIII's Oath of Obedience. In 1536, the prior

---

37 Little, 'Corrodies at the Carmelite Friary at Lynn'. Corrody: an arrangement in which an institution (e.g. a Friary) provided food and lodgings, to a lay person or people (often in their dotage) in return for a lump sum payment or the inheritance of the corrodian's property.

38 Francis, *Burnham Norton*, pp.10–11. Another example of a Carmelite connection with a river crossing was at Leighlinbridge in Ireland, where the brothers held some responsibility for the bridge (Andrews, *Other Friars*, p.25).

39 Blomefield & Parkin, *History of Norfolk*, vol. VII, p.28.

40 Burnham Overy Town's connection to the sea may have been severed before 1566, by which time there was already a 'Caunsey' (causeway) across the Burn valley downstream from it, in Burnham Norton (part of the current A149) (NRO C/Sca 1/1 m. 16–18). The port of Burnham's prosperity did not last. By the latter part of the sixteenth century, maritime trade in the Burnhams was declining in favour of neighbouring ports, with the Burnhams' largest ships only half the size of those at Wells and Cley (Hooton, 'Imagined Coastlines', pp.15–16). The port's decline was exacerbated by land reclamation schemes between the 1630s and 1822, when old staithes were cut off from the sea and more silting occurred in the Burn. The West Norfolk Junction Railway (opened 1866, running from Heacham to Wells) passed Burnham Overy Staithe by, but the cargo trade there hung on until the early twentieth century. After a long period of decline, the native oyster fishery was finished locally by 1923 (Festing, *Fishermen*, pp.79–80). Now the harbour, channel and creeks are only used by small pleasure craft.

of Burnham Norton, Robert Ryder, resigned.[41] The following year, events took a serious turn when two Burnham Norton Carmelites (William Gybson and John Pecock) were involved in the so-called Walsingham Conspiracy, an attempt to re-establish the Priory and shrine of Walsingham.[42] Both were convicted of treason; Pecock was executed in King's Lynn, whilst Gybson was sentenced to life imprisonment,[43] though later pardoned.[44] By 17 May 1538 the numbers of friars had dwindled to just four,[45] and towards the end of that month another of the Carmelites, Richard Makeyn, 'recently of Burnham Norton', was granted a dispensation to become a secular priest.[46] The Friary at Burnham Norton was dissolved later that year. The Dissolution commissioners seized the Friary's church plate, which comprised '3oz of [silver] gilt, 58oz of white and a nutt garnished with silver'.[47] So came to an end over 290 years of Carmelite presence in the Burnhams.

None of the Friary's own archive survives, and nor do the surrender and inventory documents from its dissolution. One book from the Friary is known: a commentary on the works of Aristotle of c.1476 which carries the 1511 inscription of Alanus Dersyngham, a Carmelite of Burnham.[48] Additional written material linked to the Friary is a collection of Carmelite liturgical texts, thought to have been made by a friar of Burnham Norton.[49] At the Friary site, several masonry structures still stand: the partially-restored gatehouse (Grade I listed, no. 1239045, Plates 1 & 2); part of the Friary church, later rebuilt as a barn (which itself is now ruined) (Grade II* listed, no. 1238878, Plate 3); Friary Cottage (Grade II listed, no. 1239074, Plate 4), a

41 Copsey, 'Burnham Norton: A Chronology', p.222.
42 Swales, 'Opposition to the Suppression of the Norfolk Monasteries', pp.254–65; Copsey, 'Burnham Norton: A Chronology', pp.222–3.
43 Swales, 'Opposition to the Suppression of the Norfolk Monasteries', pp.259–60.
44 L&P Hen. VIII, vol. XII(II), p.407.
45 L&P Hen. VIII, vol. XIII(I), p.374.
46 Copsey, 'Burnham Norton: A Chronology', p.223.
47 L&P Hen. VIII, vol. XVII, p.139. In this sense, 'nutt' refers to a cup or bowl made from a coconut shell with metal mounts, and 'white' probably means silver (versus silver gilt or gold), or a white-coloured alloy (OED).
48 Lablanc, Literature Criticism from 1400 to 1800, p.65.
49 Barratt, Knowing of Woman's Kind in Childing, p.17.

Plate 1. The Friary gatehouse, west façade. © The author.

Plate 2. The Friary gatehouse, east façade. © The author.

Plate 3. The remains of the Friary church's west gable,
later converted into a barn. © The author.

Plate 4. Friary Cottage *c.*1969. This view shows the cottage before it was extended westwards (to the right on the photograph). The massive limestone buttress on the cottage's north-eastern corner is visible in the centre. By 1969 the cottage had been declared unfit for human habitation by the local authority. Its renovation in 1970 saved it from dereliction. © M&F Lowe.

building developed from what might have been the infirmary, guesthouse or prior's lodgings; and large sections of the precinct wall (all discussed in Chapter 3). In contrast to the mainly urban sites of other friaries, Burnham Norton's site (Scheduled Monument no. 1013095, Fig. 2) has never been extensively developed and neither has it been systematically excavated.

Interest in the Friary was recently sparked by the Norfolk Archaeological Trust's Heritage-Lottery-Funded project, 'Imagined Land'.[50] It brought together archaeologists and archivists, a Carmelite friar (and distinguished historian of the Order), a poet, musicians, and the local community. The project resulted in many successful outcomes in very different disciplines including: a magnetometry survey of the Friary precinct; study and lecture days; test-pitting

---

[50] The 'Imagined Land' project lasted two years. Year one (2017) focused on the Tasburgh Enclosure and year two (2018) on Burnham Norton Friary.

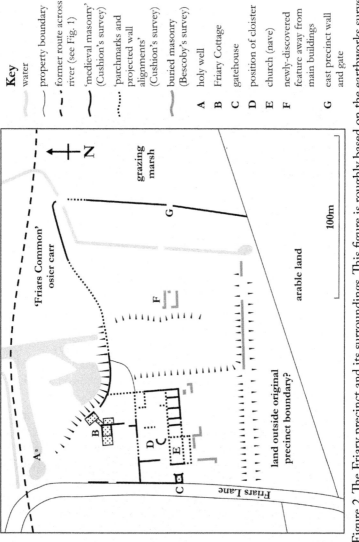

Key

水 water

—— property boundary

- - - former route across river (see Fig. 1)

⌒ 'medieval masonry' (Cushion's survey)

⋯ 'parchmarks and projected wall alignments' (Cushion's survey)

∿ buried masonry (Bescoby's survey)

A holy well

B Friary Cottage

C gatehouse

D position of cloister

E church (nave)

F newly-discovered feature away from main buildings

G east precinct wall and gate

'Friars Common' osier carr

grazing marsh

N

100m

arable land

land outside original precinct boundary?

Friars Lane

Figure 2. The Friary precinct and its surroundings. This figure is roughly based on the earthworks survey by Brian Cushion (Cushion & Davison, 'Earthworks of Norfolk'), with results from David Bescoby's magnetometry survey ('Imagined Land') and other features added by the present author. © The author.

investigations close to the site;[51] a pageant; and also the publication of a summary of existing knowledge (and new findings) about the Friary before its dissolution.[52]

Published material about Burnham Norton Friary (as well as that covering many other similar sites) has tended to concentrate on the monastic phase, paying little attention to the post-Dissolution phase, which lasted for a longer period. Therefore, almost nothing was known of the Friary's later history apart from the names of a few of its owners, and that the gatehouse had been restored and the church converted into a barn. The locations of the friars' lands, other than the precinct, were unknown, as were the post-Dissolution use and development of the site, its buildings and its former estate.

Seeing the Friary ruins today, peaceful and devoid of human activity, it is all too easy to imagine that after the Carmelites left, the site's history was over, that it was abandoned and its buildings quickly demolished. But that was not the case. This book reveals the Friary's story after 1538 by exploring two main themes: first, the Friary estate and its changing owners, and second, the fate of the Friary buildings. A brief description of the Friary's holy well is given in Appendix 1, an outline of the use of the Friary precinct as a prisoners-of-war camp in 1917 in Appendix 2, and the results of a survey of re-used ex-Friary limestone in Appendix 3. While what follows arises from a personal engagement with the site, it also coincides with renewed scholarly interest in the consequences of the Dissolution as a whole.

[51] The 'star find' from the test pits was a gilded ninth-century counter-plate from a buckle (Norfolk Archaeological Trust, *Newsletter* 19, p.5).

[52] *Burnham Norton Friary: Perspectives on the Carmelites in Norfolk*, edited by Brendan Chester-Kadwell (Norwich 2019).

2

The Friary's owners,
the Friary estate and Friar's Farm

2.1 INTRODUCTION

The Friary's estate and its changes in ownership since its Dissolution in 1538 have been little researched. While any closely-focused study such as this will have its own particularities, it may also help to illuminate and refine our wider understanding of changes in the patterns of land ownership connected to former religious houses. Moreover, by concentrating on one place it is also possible to examine those patterns over a much longer period than usually is the case.

Very brief lists of the Friary's first few holders, covering six parties in consecutive order, have been published.[1] Lists begin with an expression of interest in the site from Jane Calthorp(e) in May 1538 while the Carmelites were still living there, and end with a record of Friary 'concealed lands' in 1575/6.[2] The Friary's story is then blank for over three centuries until we leap to 1914 and learn that the site was owned by the Walpoles, Earls of Orford.[3] Now, it is part of the estate of the Coke family, Earls of Leicester. Thus, there was no information

---

[1] E.g. Blomefield & Parkin *History of Norfolk*, vol. VII, p.19; Bryant, *Churches of Norfolk*, p.22; Moore, *St Margaret's Church Burnham Norton*, p.14; Copsey, 'Burnham Norton: A Chronology', pp.224–5.

[2] Concealed lands: lands illegally detained from the Crown after leases had expired or religious houses been dissolved.

[3] Bryant, *Churches of Norfolk*, p.22.

on who owned the site, and how they used it, for 70% of the time between the Dissolution and the present day.

As well as a paucity of information on the Friary's holders, the full extent and location of its estate, namely the precinct plus its other lands, was not fully understood. The boundary wall (or its remains) on the north, east and west sides of the precinct confirm its location and approximate area (see Fig. 2). The line of its southern boundary may be indicated by the present hedge along the southern side, but it may have stood a little further to the north, where there is a slight east–west earthwork containing masonry.[4]

There is documentary evidence of three gifts of land after the Carmelites had established themselves at the Burn valley site. Their original estate or site was augmented by:

   i. 1 rood (0.25 acres) of meadow in 1298, given by Walter de Calthorp,[5]
   ii. a messuage and croft (of unknown area) in 1350, by William de Denton, chaplain,[6]
   iii. 3 acres of land in 1353, by Ralph de Femenhale (?Hemenhale) and Richard Fermen.[7]

These lands' locations are unknown, but they are thought to have been close to the Friary, with the 3 acres of 1353 possibly represented by the eastern part of the precinct, demarcated on its western edge by a linear earthwork following approximately the line of the 5m AOD (above ordnance datum) contour.[8]

---

4   Emery, 'Archaeological Surveys of the Burnham Norton Site', Fig. 4.2. The area of the precinct (1st edition OS 25 inch map Norfolk VII.3, Burnham Norton parcel 22, extending to the hedge line on the southern side) is 5.298 acres. The site and gardens of Friary Cottage (parcel 23) is 1.204 acres.

5   *CPR Edw. I*, vol. III, p.354. This is probably Sir Walter, son and heir of the one of the Friary's founders, Sir William (fl. 1241–1306) (Carr-Calthrop, *Families of Calthorpe and Calthrop*, p.29).

6   *CPR Edw. III*, vol. VIII, p.497.

7   *CPR Edw. III*, vol. IX, p.506.

8   Chester-Kadwell, 'Friary Site at Burnham Norton and its Landscape Context', pp.60–1. The datum for AOD is mean sea level at Newlyn, Cornwall.

The Friary drew income from a total of 68 acres of land: 40 acres in Burnham Norton, 14 acres in Westgate and 14 acres in Sutton, as recorded in the 1535 *Valor Ecclesiasticus*.[9] Precise locations are not given for this land, which would have been used to provide a steady source of revenue for the brethren from rents rather than having been cultivated by the Carmelites themselves.[10] The *Valor* entry for the Friary also lists eight creditors, six of which were landowning individuals or manors in the Burnhams:

i. 'Philip Calthorpe,' who was paid 7s. 11d. Probably this was the Sir Philip who held the manor of Burnham Thorpe. Its lands were in Burnhams Thorpe, Norton, Overy and Sutton.[11]

ii. 'Richard Southwell, manor of Lexham,' 2s. 7d. Lexhams manor extended into Burnhams Norton, St Andrew's, St Edmund's, Sutton, Ulph and Westgate.[12]

iii. 'Pountfrett College,' 7½d. Probably Pomfretts manor, property of the College of the Holy Trinity (Knolles Almshouse), Pontefract.[13] Blomefield does not say into which villages Pomfretts manor extended, but all references to it in the 1826 Burnham enclosure award pertain to land in Burnham Overy.[14]

iv. 'Walsingham Priory,' 12d. This priory's manor was largely in Burnham Overy, but also had lordships in Burnhams Norton and Sutton, and possibly properties in Burnham Thorpe.[15]

v. 'John Fyncham,' 19d. Two generations of John Fynchams are mentioned in relation to the manor of Deepdale. 'John Finham' [*sic*] died possessed of the manor of Deepdale during Henry VIII's reign, and his grandson 'William Fincham' the

---

9   *Valor Ecclesiasticus*, vol. III, p.371 (translated in Copsey, 'Burnham Norton: A Chronology', p.222). There has been a temptation to interpret these figures as proof that the friars *owned* 68 acres of land (e.g. in Pierssené, 'Burnham Norton Friary').

10 Richard Copsey pers. comm., 1 October 2020; Susanna Wade-Martins pers. comm., 4 November 2020.

11 'Burnham Inclosure Award 1826'.

12 Blomefield & Parkin, *History of Norfolk*, vol. VII, pp.16, 30, 31, 36.

13 Blomefield & Parkin, *History of Norfolk*, vol. VII, p.21.

14 But see Table 2.

15 Blomefield & Parkin, *History of Norfolk*, vol. VII, pp.16, 24, 30.

same in Elizabeth I's. The manor's lands were in Burnhams Deepdale, Norton, Sutton, Ulph and Westgate.[16]

vi. 'Burnham Norton church,' 8d.

vii. 'House of St. John of Carbrooke,' 1d. This refers to a Norfolk Preceptory of Knights Hospitallers, but it is not known whether they held any land in the Burnhams.

viii. 'Hugh Thurlowe,' 2d. Probably he of Burnham Ulph, a local landowner who died in 1569.[17]

The payment to the church may have been to cover a perpetual candle at a grave, and to say masses,[18] or a rent. Perhaps the single penny paid to Carbrooke was a simple donation.

Documentary and toponymic research into the Friary has produced a deeper understanding of the sequence of owners and their changes, and of information on the Friary estate. A new and expanded list of owners is presented below (2.2), with more detail about each party and the Friary estate during each of their ownerships or tenancies (2.3). Friary-related toponyms (place-names) in the Burnhams are recorded and analysed in Section 2.4. All the new findings are drawn together and discussed in Section 2.5.

2.2 SUMMARY OF POST-DISSOLUTION OWNERS OF THE FRIARY

New research into archival sources and a single secondary source has revealed the succession of historical holders or owners of the Friary, together with people who had interests in it (summarised in Table 1).

---

[16] NRO Hare 598, 187X6; Blomefield & Parkin, *History of Norfolk*, vol. VII, p.9.

[17] Debrett, *Peerage*, vol. I, p.537.

[18] Richard Copsey pers. comm., 1 October 2020.

Table 1. Expressions of interest in, and ownership and tenancy of, the Friary during and after the Dissolution.

Phase and date(s)	Names & details
I. May 1538	Lady Jane Calthorpe attempts to buy Friary while Carmelites still in residence
II. Late 1538/9 to 1541	The Crown, with preferment given to Richard Gresham (tenants: Lady Jane Calthorpe, Robert Boston, Oliver Remes)
III. 1541 to 1544	George Lord Cobham & Edward Warner (tenants: Lady Jane Calthorpe, Robert Boston, Oliver Remes)
IV. 1544 to 1545	Lady Jane Calthorpe (tenants: Robert Boston, Oliver Remes)
V. 1545 to 1561	William & Anne Blennerhasset (later, second wife Alice)
VI. Jan 1561 to ?	John Hall & Richard Norton
VII. Nov 1561 to 1566	William Bromefelde or Bromfield (later William Bromfield junior) & Thomas Pepes or Pepys
VIII. 1566 to no later than 1583	Robert Jenyson (d. *c.*1583)
IX. 15?? to probably no later than 1600	Southwell family of St Faith's
X. ? to 1576	Francis Cobbe (d. 1582)
XI. 1570 to ?	Nicholas Mynne & John Hall (concealed lands, tenant: John Wightman)
XII. 1575 to ?	John Herbert & Andrew Palmer (concealed lands, tenant: Robert Jenyson)
XIII. 1576 to ?	Edward Grymeston senior & Edward Grymeston junior (concealed land, tenant: Francis Cobbe)
XIV. ? to 1616/17	Sir Charles Cornwallis
XV. 1616/17 to ?	Thomas Sturges
XVI. No later than 1619 to no later than 1673	Sir Stephen Soame (d. 1619), later son John Soame, presumably afterwards grandson John Soame (d. 1673)
XVII. 1673 to no later than 1675	Sir William Palmer
XVIII. ? to 1675	Thomas Savile & Hugh Myddleton
XIX. 1675 to ?	Thomas Tyndall

(cont.)

Table 1 (cont.)

Phase and date(s)	Names & details
XX. ? to 1689	Hugh Myddleton & Bartholomew Soame (tenants: formerly Edmund Lyme or Lynne, later Clement Woodrow, and Widow Harris)
XXI. 1689 to 1690	John Goldsmith & William Appleford as trustees for Dame Dorothea Myddleton (same tenants)
XXII. 1690 (or c.1706) to 1723	Sir John Smith (tenants: Bacon Hibgame, later Clement Woodrowe & John Hibgame & Widow Harris)
XXIII. ? to 1700	John Weddell in trust for John Harris and heirs
XXIV. 1723 to 1725	Peter Lombard (d. 1725) (tenants same as under Smith)
XXV. 1725 to 1922	Horatio 1st Baron Walpole and descendants (Earls of Orford) (tenants: Catherine Hibgame, next Thomas Foley, later William Mack, later John Savory)
XXVI. 1922 to present day	Thomas William Coke, 3rd Earl of Leicester, and descendants (1968 Friary Cottage sold to Philips family) (C20th onwards tenants of the former precinct: Mr Shearar, John Smith, the Norfolk Archaeological Trust)

2.3 THE PARTIES AND THE ESTATE IN DETAIL

Phase I. Calthorpe

The first expression of interest in the Friary during the Dissolution was from a prominent local family, the Calthorpes, descendants of one of the Friary's original founders. Burnham Thorpe manor had been in the Calthorpes' possession since the time of Henry III,[19] and in 1511, Lady Jane Calthorpe, and her male heirs by her husband Sir Philip, were also granted Polstead Hall manor,[20] which extended into Burnhams Westgate and Norton.[21] The Calthorpes had important

[19] Blomefield & Parkin, *History of Norfolk*, vol. VII, p.12.
[20] *L&P Hen. VIII*, vol. XIX(I), p.80.
[21] Lady Jane Calthorpe (née Blennerhasset: Blomefield & Parkin, *History of Norfolk*, vol. VI, p.518; *ODNB*, 'Radcliffe, Egremont, d. 1578') appears as Lady Joan in some sources. For better clarity, she remains Jane Calthorpe throughout this book. Sir Philip Calthorpe was the eighth generation descendant and heir of one of the Friary's original founders (Blomefield &

roles in the household of Henry VIII.[22] Philip Calthorpe was the Friary's principal creditor in 1535.[23]

Lady Jane was widowed in spring 1535. Her stepson, Philip the younger (son of Sir Philip's first wife, Mary Say)[24] inherited his father's five Suffolk and ten Norfolk manors (though not Polstead Hall). The relationship between Lady Jane and the young Philip seems to have been unhappy: only two years later, they were in legal dispute over parts of the Calthorpe estate.[25] Lady Jane perhaps viewed the Dissolution as an opportunity to secure more property for herself and thus break free from any dependency on her stepson. On 17 May 1538 she wrote to 'Cromwell' (presumably Thomas Cromwell, orchestrator of the Dissolution) asking to purchase the Friary near her Polstead Hall manor. She stated that there were only four friars, 'in so grete povertie' that they could not afford to sustain the house, which was 'not unlyke within short tyme to Fall in grete ruyne and decay.' She explained she had nowhere 'to inhabite my self in but oonly oon pore howse in Norwich from the which I am dyverse tymes inforced to Flee by cause of the plage [plague]'.[26] It appears that Lady

Parkin, *History of Norfolk*, vol. VI, pp.515–8; Lee-Warner, 'The Calthorpes of Burnham'). Spellings for the manors' names are standardised here as in The National Archives' Manorial Documents Register.

22 The Calthorpe family was well-connected: Sir Philip attended the 1514 wedding of the Princess Mary (to Louis XII of France: *L&P Hen. VIII*, vol. I, p.898), and in 1521 was appointed by Henry VIII as chamberlain in the royal household, with Lady Jane as governess to the young Mary Tudor (*ODNB*, 'Mary I, 1516–1558'). Their names appear many times in the Letters and Papers of Henry VIII.

23 *Valor Ecclesiasticus*, vol. III, p.371.

24 Blomefield & Parkin, *History of Norfolk*, vol. VI, p.518; Carr-Calthrop, *Families of Calthorpe and Calthrop*, p.47.

25 *L&P Hen. VIII*, vol. XII(I), p.531.

26 *L&P Hen. VIII*, vol. XIII(I), p.374; TNA SP 1/132, fol. 101. The Calthorpe's Norwich house was hardly 'pore': it was Berney's Inn, a 'spacious mansion' in St Martin's parish, bought by Sir Philip's ancestor in 1447/8 (Druery, 'Erpingham House', pp.143, 145). This building reportedly contained a chestnut-panelled banqueting room of 17 × 35ft with a 10-foot south facing window; it survived until 1858 (*ibid.*, p.146). Whether Lady Jane lived there immediately after her husband's death is not known, but it was her residence in 1548/9 (*ibid.*, p.145). She died in 1550 (Carr-Calthrop, *Families of Calthorpe and Calthrop*, p.48).

Jane's intention may have been to use or convert the still-intact Friary buildings into some kind of rural bolt-hole. No reply from Cromwell to Lady Jane is known to have survived.

Phase II. The Crown (Friary site & portion of lands)

The exact date when the Carmelites departed is unknown, but by the latter part of 1538 presumably the Friary was empty. It was not 'defasede ne rasede' [defaced nor razed], maybe because of lobbying by Lady Jane Calthorpe, and:

> ... the howses ther be not solde but stond still as theye ware lefte by the Vysitor by cawse of a Certeyn leter writen by Mr Southwell unto Willyam Buttes his deput[y] ther that he sholde in no case medell with no part of the same house in makinge of Enye salle by cawse that Sir Richarde Gressehame Knyght hathe the preferment of the sayde howse at the kinges hand as Mr Southwell doth wryte.[27]

Sir Richard Gresham, mercer and merchant adventurer, was born in Holt (Norfolk), c.1485. He became Lord Mayor of London in 1537. In 1538, he entered that novel, highly lucrative market of buying former monastic properties all over England, asset-stripping them, especially of their metals, and selling them on at huge profit.[28] Though the lead roofs were still *in situ* at the Friary in 1541,[29] by 1543, the bells of Burnham Norton and Blakeney Carmelite Friaries had been sold by Gresham.[30]

As attested by accounts from 1539–40, Lady Calthorpe paid 27s. 4½d. for the former house of friars in Burnham. Another set of accounts gives more detail of the house and possessions of the former

---

[27] *L&P Hen. VIII*, vol. XIII(II), p.508 (letter of 1538, but undated); TNA SP 5/4/152, fol. 126.

[28] *ODNB*, 'Gresham, Sir Richard, c.1485–1549'.

[29] TNA C66/708 mm. 32–3.

[30] *L&P Hen. VIII*, vol. XVIII(II), p.119. Later, Sir Henry Spelman had very strong views on the results of the sacrilege of the Dissolution and in particular the unhappy fates of people involved. He related his childhood memories of bells being removed all over Norfolk, and 'that in sending them overseas, some were drowned in one haven, some in another as at Lynn, Wells, or Yarmouth' (*History of Sacrilege*, p.258).

Friary, revealing that Lady Jane Calthorpe (erroneously referred to as Lady Anne Calthorpe, widow)[31] had the tenancy and occupation of:

   i. the site, gardens, orchards etc. of the former Friary (rent: 6s. 8d.),
   ii. 32 acres of arable land (rent: 13s. 7½d.),
   iii. 1 rood (0.25 acres) of land near the Friary gatehouse (rent: 4d.).[32]

Oliver Remes was the tenant of 2½ acres of additional Friary land called 'le Ashe pyghtell'[33] (rent: 6s. 8d.), and Robert Bostons held 3 acres called 'Vyncentes' (rent: 10s.). The total measured area of lands is 37 acres & 3 roods (37.75 acres), a long way short of the pre-Dissolution figure of 68 acres. The shortfall cannot be made up by the unmeasured Friary site/precinct, item (i) above, which, depending on its original boundaries, contained *c.*6.5 acres (6 acres & 2 roods). This means that close to half of the friars' original estate was now in unknown hands.

Out of the total rents received for the former Friary and its lands, the following dues were paid to:

   i. Lady 'Anne Calthorpe' at the manor of Polstead Hall (2s. 6d.),
   ii. Philip Calthorpe at the manor of Burnham Thorpe (15d.),
   iii. 'Elysabeth Calthorpe'[34] at the manor of Haklowe [Hall Close] (10d.),
   iv. Richard Southwell at the manor of Lexhams (2s. 7d.),

---

[31] This is probably a mistake by the scribe, as no widowed Anne Calthorpes can be traced during this period with any connection to the local area. According to Rye (*Visitacion of Norfolk*, p.64), Anne or Amy Bullyne married Sir Philip Calthorpe junior (stepson of Lady Jane Calthorpe). It is assumed Sir Philip Calthorpe junior is Sir Philip Calthorpe of Erwarton (Suffolk), whose will dates to 1552 (TNA PROB 11/35/71), meaning that this Lady Anne was not a widow in 1541. A second person named Anne Calthorpe was the youngest daughter of Sir Philip senior and Lady Jane (Rye, *Visitacion of Norfolk*, p.64). This Anne married Henry, Earl of Sussex, but he divorced her (Carr-Calthrop, *Families of Calthorpe and Calthrop*, p.48).

[32] TNA SC 6/HENVIII/7438 rot. 9; TNA SC 6/HENVIII/2632 rot. 54d–55a.

[33] 'Pightle': the dialect word for a small field or piece of enclosed land.

[34] This might be the unmarried daughter of Sir Philip Calthorpe senior from his first marriage, i.e. Lady Jane's stepdaughter (Carr-Calthrop, *Families*

    v. The priests of 'Pomfrete' College at the manor of Knolles [Pomfretts manor] (7½d.),

   vi. John Fynchame at the manor of 'Shooldhames' in Deepdale (18d.),[35]

  vii. The Rectory of Norton (8d.).

Some of the above names are identical to those in the *Valor*'s 1535 list of creditors and are analysed more fully in the Discussion. That the friars had now gone, but many of the creditors were still being paid shows that these payments cannot all have been for the friars' food or fuel: they must have been rents. The post-Dissolution Friary estate (37 acres & 3 roods plus the precinct) therefore probably comprised lands that the Carmelites had been given (their endowed lands), together with lands they had rented from local landowners and then sub-let to their own tenants. To the long list of roles the Friary played in the local community (p.7) may therefore be added one more: rural landlord.

Phase III. Cobham (Brooke) and Warner (Friary site & portion of lands)

The Friary site was granted to George Lord Cobham (George Brooke, 9th Baron Cobham, *c*.1497–1558) and Edward Warner (1511–1565; knighted 1544), and the heirs and assignees of Warner, on 24 May 1541.[36] Lady Jane now paid 3s. 8d. directly to the Crown in connection with the Friary, but no dues were recorded to the seven creditors listed above.[37]

    Warner later married Elizabeth Brooke, sister of Lord Cobham, making him and the baron brothers-in-law. It is unknown why Cobham and Warner were chosen to receive the Friary, but Cobham,

---

    of Calthorpe and Calthrop, pp.47–8). Hall Close was not one of the manors inherited by Sir Philip junior from his father.

35 This is Deepdale manor, held by Thomas Shouldham until 1467 (Blomefield & Parkin, *History of Norfolk*, vol. VII, p.9).

36 *L&P Hen. VIII*, vol. XVI, p.426; TNA C66/708 mm. 32–3; Hofmann, 'Warner, Sir Edward (1511–65)'. Some sources (including Bryant, *Churches of Norfolk*, p.22) incorrectly state that the site went to William (1527–1597), the 10th Baron Cobham and son of George, but William would only have been a child in 1541 and there is no reason to suppose that the original 1541 licence, naming George, is incorrect.

37 TNA SC 6/HENVIII/2633 rot. 49a; TNA SC 6/HENVIII/7439 rot. 1.

a soldier and landowner based in Kent, was the recipient of much former monastic property at the Dissolution.[38] Warner, a soldier and a protestant, was born at Besthorpe (Norfolk)[39] and, it turns out, was a nephew of Lady Jane Calthorpe.[40] Entering the King's Household in 1537, Warner was an 'active dealer in monastic property, selling or exchanging nearly as much as he bought'.[41]

In 1541, the Friary's roofing lead was part of the grant to Cobham and Warner. The premises was all in 'Burneham' and now consisted of:

   i. The house and site of the former Friary, specifically, the church, bell tower and cemetery ... messuages, houses, buildings, orchards, gardens, land & soil,

   ii. 3 acres of land with a house on it,

   iii. 1 rood (0.25 acres) of pasture with a stable, opposite the gate of the Friary,

   iv. 2½ acres of land called 'Le Asshe Pightell' (tenant, Oliver Remes),

   v. 2 acres of enclosed pasture called 'Vyncentes Close' (tenant, Robert Boston),

   vi. 32 acres & ⅓ rood (32.0833 acres) of arable lands lying separately in separate fields of 'Burneham'.[42]

That the Friary had a bell tower (see Section 3.6), not just a modest bell-cote, is a new discovery.

All those houses, chambers, buildings, grounds, orchards and gardens within the site and precinct, as well as items (ii) & (iii) were, in 1541, now or late in the tenure of Lady 'Anne Calthorpe,' widow, i.e. Lady Jane Calthorpe. The Friary estate now measured 39 acres &

38 *ODNB*, 'Brooke, George, ninth Baron Cobham (*c*.1497–1558)'.

39 *ODNB*, 'Warner, Sir Edward (1511–1565)'.

40 Blomefield, *History of Norfolk*, vol. I, pp.497–8.

41 Hofmann, 'Warner, Sir Edward (1511–65)'.

42 TNA C66/708 mm. 32–3. In this historical context, 'Burneham' (or Burnham) means all or any of the parishes comprising the Burnhams. This includes Burnhams Norton, Sutton, Westgate, Ulph, Overy (Overy Town and Overy Staithe), Thorpe and Deepdale (all usually referred to by their last names locally), plus the lost parishes of St Edmund's and St Andrew's. Modern-day Burnham Market comprises Westgate, Sutton and Ulph and today is called 'Burnham'.

3⅓ roods (39.8333 acres) because of small differences in given acreages for items (v) and (vi) and the addition to the list of item (ii).

Phase IV. Calthorpe (Friary site & portion of lands)

In 1544, it appears that the nephew and aunt, Warner and Lady Jane, made a swap. On 14 February, Polstead Hall manor and 3 acres of land in 'Westhowe field' in Burnham were granted to Warner, to take possession after Lady Jane, who held them for life.[43] One week later, Brooke (Lord Cobham) and Warner were granted a licence (costing 11s.) to alienate to one 'lady Anne Calthorp', widow (again, Lady Jane), the Friary lands and buildings.[44] Their description was the same as in 1541, except that no mention was now made of any roofing lead, woods or underwoods.

Phase V. Blennerhasset (Friary site & portion of lands)

On 8 November 1545, 'Joan Calthorp, widow', i.e. Lady Jane, was granted her licence (for 11s. 1½d.) to alienate the Friary and its lands to 'William Blenerhayset' (William Blennerhasset: another of her nephews)[45] and Anne his wife.[46] Blennerhasset lived near Norwich, first at Horsford and later at Pockthorpe.[47] He became tenant of the Pockthorpe house (The Lathes, later called Hassett's House) after Lady Jane transferred her lease of it to him.[48]

The property's description was as in 1544 except that only the 3 acres and its house was then 'in the farm of' Lady Jane. As late as 1547, she was still paying 3s. 8d. annually to the Crown, being the holder of a 'tenth part' of the Friary premises.[49]

43 *L&P Hen. VIII*, vol. XIX(I), p.80.
44 *L&P Hen. VIII*, vol. XIX(I), p.85; TNA C66/725 m. 16. In NRO C/Sca 1/1 mm. 16–18 it is claimed that Cobham had granted the site solely to Warner on 8 December in Henry VIII's 32nd regnal year (December 1540). This cannot be correct because Cobham and Warner themselves were not granted the Friary until May 1541, and Cobham's and Warner's names were on the grant to Lady Jane Calthorpe in 1544.
45 Rye, *Visitacion of Norfolk*, p.39.
46 *L&P Hen. VIII*, vol. XX(II), p.454; TNA C66/784 m. 4.
47 Montgomery-Massingberd, *Burke's Irish Family Records*, pp.134–5.
48 Bulwer, 'Hassett's House, Norwich'.
49 TNA SC 6/HENVIII/7441 rot. 10.

Phase VI. Hall and Norton (portion of Friary lands only?)

Blennerhasset was widowed after 1545 and subsequently married Alice Sibseye.[50] This couple 'assured the [Friary] premises', plus an 11-acre marsh called 'Martyndales' (in either Burnham Norton or Overy judging by its description) and 1½ acres of arable land at 'Kyrkedale' in Burnham Overy to John Hall and Richard Norton, by an indenture dated 14 January 1561 (now lost).[51] With no more details, it is unclear whether Hall and Norton were given a lease that reverted back to the Blennerhassets (possibly after only a few months; see next entry) or how much of the former Friary estate they took over. Martyndales and the Kyrkedale land appear to be post-Dissolution additions to the estate.

Phase VII. Bromefelde and Pepes (Friary site & portion of lands)

On 24 November 1561, William 'Blenerhayset' (Blennerhasset), Gent., was granted a licence (for 11s. 1½d.) to alienate the house, site and church of the Carmelites, and lands, to William Bromefelde, Esq. and Thomas Pepes, Gent.[52] Bromefelde has not been traced, but Pepes was probably the son of John Pepys of South Creake (Norfolk), merchant, who inherited Roses manor there. John Pepys was linked to the Calthorpes, being a tenant of 'Philip Calthorp' the younger in 1539.[53]

---

[50] NRO S/Ca 1/1 mm. 16–18; Rye, *Visitacion of Norfolk*, p.39.

[51] NRO S/Ca 1/1 mm. 16–18. The marsh was formerly Edward Martyndale's, and was 'betwene the Mill Caunsey [causeway] in Burnham Norton on the West And the marsshe of the parson of Burnham Norton on the East And the North hedd abbutteth uppon the Myll Damme And the Sowth hedd abbutteth uppo[n] the kinges high way called Scowtergate' (*ibid.*). Martyndale lived at the site of Pomfretts manor in Burnham Overy in Mary I's reign (Blomefield & Parkin, *History of Norfolk*, vol. VII, p.21).

[52] *CPR Eliz. I*, vol. II, p.369; TNA C66/984 m. 6. Blomefield & Parkin (*History of Norfolk*, vol. VII, p.19) claim that the licence was granted to John Blennerhasset, but William's name occurs in the original document, and there is nothing to suggest that this is a mistake.

[53] *L&P Hen. VIII*, vol. XIV(I), p.556. Thomas Pepys lived until 1569 and was buried at South Creake (Blomefield & Parkin, *History of Norfolk*, vol. VII, pp.80–1). He was distantly related to the diarist, Samuel and the former's branch of the family was referred to by the latter as 'my Norfolk cousins' (Moore, *St Margaret's Church Burnham Norton*, p.14).

It may be that 1561 saw another splitting up of the Friary estate, with part of it being disposed of in January (to Hall and Norton), and the remainder in November (to Bromefelde and Pepes). If this were so, it seems odd that the Friary's physical description in the November licence was the same as it was in 1544 (except that woods and underwoods were included again). In November 1561 Blennerhasset was the tenant of the house on the 3-acre site and of Le Asshe Pightell, whilst Robert Boston retained Vyncentes Close as before.

Phase VIII. Jenyson (portion of Friary lands only)

We move forward to 10 April 1566, when William Bromefelde's heir, also William (of Sustead, Norfolk) and Thomas Pepys of South Creake conveyed lands in Burnhams Norton, Westgate and Deepdale, formerly the friars', to Robert Jenyson of Burnham Westgate.[54] Jenyson was a significant local landowner, having purchased Hall Close and Games manors in Burnham Overy, church advowsons, messuages (dwelling houses with outbuildings and land), (arable) land, pasture, meadow, wood, heath and marsh, plus a water mill, making an estate that extended throughout the Burnhams. He also held other quite extensive lands in Burnham Westgate.[55] Jenyson died in c.1583.[56]

The 1566 indenture's recital summarises previous transfers of the lands, including to 'ladye Jane Calthorp late the wief [*sic*] of Sir Philip Calthorpe deceased' and replicates the sequence of owners above from Phases *III* to *VII*, but it does not refer to the premises in the same way as the original grant and subsequent licences up to 1561. For instance, there is no mention of the friars' former church, Friary buildings and precinct, nor the 3 acres with the house, the 1 rood with the stable, and Le Asshe Pightell. This detailed comparison shows that the Friary estate was fragmented either by the 1566 sale, or before.

Jenyson's indenture precisely describes the location of Vyncentes Close: '... adioning unto the kings High[way] that ledeth from the parisshe of Saint Andrewes unto the late dissolved howse or Pryory called the Fryers Carmellettes on the Est and the Closse of John

---

54 Tingey, 'Calendar of Deeds', p.50; NRO CScai/1 mm. 16–18.
55 Blomefield & Parkin, *History of Norfolk*, vol. VII, pp.22, 35.
56 NRO MS 3254, 4B1.

Boston on the West and abutteth upon the kynges high way upon the So[uth]'.[57]

The indenture's schedule details an additional 58 acres & ¼ rood (58.0625 acres) of land. The land is in 73 parcels, of which twelve are unambiguously listed under the heading 'The Land of the late Fryers within the feyld of Burnham Westgate', and the frequent references to the friars throughout the schedule imply that the rest of the land was also part of the Friary estate. Notice the large increase in acreage compared with the figures in the Cobham and Warner grant (39 acres & 3⅓ roods (39.8333 acres)), described above.

An examination of the place-names used in these documents is itself revealing. Jenyson's schedule contains the earliest documentary evidence for springs associated with the Friary: the first item listed being 'Spryng Wells Yarde', which abutted the west side of Friars Lane. See Appendix 1 for more detail on the springs and holy well. Another toponym that particularly stands out is 'the Stey late Carmestye which ledeth from the howse of the late Fryers to Burnham Depedale'. Carmestye (sty = a path or narrow way (OED);[58] Carmestye = Carmel sty?) has now gone but was probably the western section of the old route which ran from the Burnham Deepdale Road across the Burn valley, past the Friary, to Burnham Overy Town (see Fig. 1). It was stopped up by the enclosure in 1826.[59]

Fifteen of the 73 parcels of land (roughly 20% of them) abutted Carmestye and they were spread over four different furlongs (divisions within a larger unenclosed field). Carmestye is a term unknown and unused today, but it occurred in a documentary source as late as 1922: a schedule of copyhold hereditaments of Burnham Windhams manor, one detail from a sale of properties that included the Friary site (see Phase *XXVI*, below).[60]

Other toponyms for, or associated with, the Friary lands in Burnham Norton included: 'Parsonage Closse' [*sic*], 'Countes Acre',

---

57 NRO CScar/1 mm. 16–18.

58 Especially a footpath that ascended a hill (Candler, 'East Anglian Field-Names', p.174; Hesse, 'Fields, Tracks and Boundaries in the Creakes', p.305), which Carmestye does as it passes by Burnham Norton church.

59 Only a short section of it appears to have been still in regular use by 1797 according to Faden's map (Barringer, *Faden's Map of Norfolk*).

60 Holkham Hall Archives, 'Conveyance between the Earl of Orford and the Earl of Leicester. 8 June 1922'.

'Mill Stey Way', 'Fowlde Acre', 'Scarte Acre', 'Hegges Yard', 'Berestye',[61]
'Roptell', 'Bradmere' (location known), 'Brandon Mere' (meer or
mere = a boundary or border (OED): here the boundary between
Burnhams Norton and Westgate), 'Sandepytt Furlong', 'Pitterkyns'
(named after its previous owner), 'Cosynstey', 'Moreblades',[62] 'Dowes
Acre', 'Breneshowe', 'Oldhowe' and 'Puttockes Hill'. Toponyms used
in conjunction with the Burnham Westgate land were 'Fetherell Stey',
'Brandon Mere' and 'Heigh Brandon'.

Phase IX. Southwell (Friary site & portion of lands?)

No record has been found of the disposal of the Friary site by
Bromefelde/Bromfield and Pepys. There is now a gap in the primary
documentary sources, and we turn to a secondary source in the form
of Sir Henry Spelman (*c.*1564–1641) for information on this, and
Phases *X*, *XIV* and *XVI*. This Norfolk landowner and antiquarian
wrote *The History and Fate of Sacrilege* in *c.*1632; it was first published
in 1698, reprinted in the nineteenth century, and it includes lists of
post-Dissolution owners of Norfolk's religious houses. 'The Southwells
of St Faith's' were first in the list of Burnham Norton Friary owners
compiled by Spelman.[63] The Southwells occupied the dissolved
Benedictine priory at Horsham St Faith's near Norwich, which was
first granted to Sir Richard Southwell (of Woodrising in Norfolk,
and London; 1502/3–1564; knighted 1540) in 1538.[64] Sir Richard
also held Burnham Lexhams manor in Burnham Westgate,[65] and

---

[61] The similar toponym 'Beer Stye' in East Anglia has been interpreted
as meaning 'Bier Sty', probably a pathway to a church (Candler, 'East
Anglian Field-Names', p.173). Another example of this is in South Creake
(Norfolk), of which Mary Hesse writes: 'Biersty' alias 'Kirksty' is clearly a
funeral way from ... the village to the church' ('Medieval Field Systems
in South Creake', p.85). 'Berestye' in Burnham Norton might therefore
be the road between the main village and the parish church (a section
of the A149 leading to part of the B1355), which, in the same manner as
other 'sty' routes, ascends a hill.

[62] Moreblades was 24 acres in extent in 1805 (NRO MC 18809, 100X2).

[63] Spelman, *History of Sacrilege*, p.252.

[64] Blomefield & Parkin, *History of Norfolk*, vol. X, p.440; *ODNB*, 'Southwell,
Sir Richard (1502/3–1564)'; Swales, 'Redistribution of Monastic Lands in
Norfolk', p.22.

[65] Blomefield & Parkin, *History of Norfolk*, vol. VII, p.37.

in that role he was one of the Friary's creditors in the *Valor*. He was intimately involved with the Dissolution, being receiver for the Court of Augmentations for Norfolk and Suffolk (1536–42), commissioner for the survey of the two counties' monasteries (1537), and commissioner for suppression (1539).[66] More than 30 Norfolk manors and over 10,000 sheep were in his possession when he died.[67] Most of Sir Richard's lands were inherited by his nearest legitimate male heir, his nephew Thomas Southwell,[68] who went on to sell Polstead Hall and Burnham Lexhams manors, but not the Friary, in 1602.[69]

Spelman may well have meant not Sir Richard Southwell, but his first illegitimate son, Richard Southwell *alias* Darcy, who inherited St Faith's from his father in 1545.[70] This younger Richard was a barrister and briefly an MP. He died in the Fleet prison in 1600.[71] There is no corroborating evidence for the Southwells' ownership or tenure of the Friary, but dates indicate that they could have bought the site from Bromefelde/Bromfield and Pepys.

Phase X. Cobbe (Friary site & portion of lands?)

Spelman's list gives 'Francis Cobbes' as the next owner of the Friary after the Southwells.[72] Francis Cobbe, Gent., of Burnham Norton, held part of Polstead Hall manor in 1573/4, the manor of Donnells (or Danyels) in Burnham Sutton, plus lands and 'wreck of sea' in Burnham Norton

---

66 Virgoe, 'Southwell, Richard (1502/3–64), of London and Wood Rising, Norf'. Court of Augmentations: Henry VIII's new administrative body responsible for ex-religious property.

67 *ODNB*, 'Southwell, Sir Richard (1502/3–1564)'.

68 Johnson, 'Southwell, alias Darcy, Richard (by 1531–1600)'.

69 NRO BRA 664/1, 815X1. Thomas Southwell sold Polstead Hall and Lexhams manors and local church patronages to Thomas Rowse, Thomas Rychardson and John Payne in 1602. 'Thomas Rouse' later had a praecipe (a writ designed to elicit an immediate action) to render Polstead Hall manor to Henry Cornwallis and Robert Drury (Blomefield & Parkin, *History of Norfolk*, vol. VII, p.35).

70 Johnson, 'Southwell, alias Darcy, Richard (by 1531–1600)'. The manor and rectory of 'St Faith' was settled by Sir Richard on the mother of Richard Southwell (*alias* Darcy) in 1544 (Swales, 'Redistribution of Monastic Lands in Norfolk', p.22).

71 Johnson, 'Southwell, alias Darcy, Richard (by 1531–1600)'.

72 Spelman, *History of Sacrilege*, p.252.

from 1575.[73] A Francis Cobbe (of Burnham Sutton) was related to the above mentioned Jenyson family, having married Margaret, Robert Jenyson's eldest half-sister.[74] Cobbe could have acquired Friary land through his in-laws. Cobbe was buried at Burnham Norton in 1582. He was the only one of the Friary's many post-Dissolution owners that lived in the parish in which the Friary is located.

Cobbe had been a tenant of 2 acres of concealed lands in Burnham Norton once belonging to the Carmelites, and later granted to 'Edward Grymston' (see Phase *XIII*, below).[75]

Phase XI. Mynne and Hall (Friary concealed lands)

Archival sources show that in the 1570s, there was a series of grants in fee simple (a form of freehold ownership) of concealed lands that once belonged to the friars. The first, on 9 February 1570, for £180, was to Nicholas Mynne of Little Walsingham (Norfolk) and John Hall the younger of North Barsham (Norfolk), and the heirs and assigns of Mynne. It is not known whether the 'John Hall' of this Phase is the same man as in Phase *VI*. Mynne had another connection to the Burnhams: he gave part of the tithes of Burnham Overy (once belonging to Wymondham Priory, Norfolk) to Gonville and Caius College, Cambridge.[76]

The 1570 grant comprised many lands in Norfolk and other counties, including 2 acres of concealed marshes in 'Burneham' originally possessed by the Friary.[77] Their annual value was 8d., and their tenant was John Wightman.

Phase XII. Herbert and Palmer (Friary concealed lands)

On 22 September 1575, lands all over the country were granted to John Herbert and Andrew Palmer, citizen and goldsmith of London,

---

73 Blomefield & Parkin, *History of Norfolk*, vol. VII, pp.34, 29; *CPR Eliz. I*, vol. VII, p.402. 'Wreck of sea' was a right to salvage vessels and goods cast up on the shore.

74 Rye, *Visitacion of Norfolk*, p.172.

75 Blomefield & Parkin, *History of Norfolk*, vol. VII, p.19. Cobbe purchased certain properties in Burnham Norton (but not the Friary site) from the Pepys family in 1565/6 (NRO S/Ca 1/1 mm. 42–42d).

76 Bryant, *Churches of Norfolk*, p.43; Caius, *Annals of Gonville and Caius*, p.178.

77 *CPR Eliz. I*, vol. V, p.43; TNA C66/1063 m. 16.

at the request of 'John Perott', knight, 'for £397 5s. paid by him at the Exchequer; and for his service'.[78] Sir John Perrot had been a commissioner for concealed lands, was a Privy Councillor to Elizabeth I and had links to Sir William Herbert, 1st Earl of Pembroke.[79] Palmer was probably the Andrew Palmer who was the first secretary of the Company of Mineral and Battery Works (which had a monopoly to make various metal goods) and later, deputy controller of the Royal Mint.[80]

The grant included 16 acres of land in the fields of Burnhams Westgate, St Andrew's and 'Digdale' [Deepdale] late of the house of Carmelite friars of Burnham Norton.[81] This was in the tenure of 'Robert Jennyson,' the owner of much Friary land in Phase *VIII*.

Phase XIII. Grymeston (Friary concealed lands)

The following year on 28 November, 2 acres of enclosed land in Burnham Norton, formerly the friars', now or late in the tenure of Francis Cobbe, was part of an enormous grant of property in Norfolk and elsewhere to Edward Grymeston and his son and heir, also Edward for, £172 6s.[82] The identity of the Grymestons is uncertain, for theirs was not a local name in the Burnhams. Bearing in mind the total extent and wide geographical spread of their newly granted lands, they could have been important establishment figures. They might have been Edward Grimston (1507/8–1600) of Rishangles in Suffolk, former comptroller of Calais, and his eponymous son.[83]

Phase XIV. Cornwallis (Friary site & some lands apparently re-united)

According to Spelman, Sir Charles Cornwallis held the Friary after Cobbe, but 'wasted' the estate (stripped it of its assets).[84] Cornwallis (c.1555–1629; knighted 1603; second son of Sir Thomas Cornwallis of Brome Hall, Suffolk) also held Polstead Hall and Burnham

---

[78] *CPR Eliz. I*, vol. VI, p.408.

[79] Edwards, 'Perrot (Parret), John (1528/29–92)'.

[80] M.R.P., 'Palmer, Andrew (c.1544–1599)'.

[81] *CPR Eliz. I*, vol. VI, pp.413–4; TNA C66/1125 m. 30.

[82] *CPR Eliz. I*, vol. VII, p.284; TNA C66/1155 m. 12.

[83] Thrush, 'Grimston, Sir Harbottle, 1st Bt. (c.1578–1648)'; J.H., 'Grimston, Edward (c.1508–1600)'; *ODNB*, 'Grimston, Edward (1507/8–1600)'.

[84] Spelman, *History of Sacrilege*, p.252.

Deepdale manors during Elizabeth I's reign.[85] He was an MP, resident ambassador to Spain until 1609, and later treasurer to the household of Henry, Prince of Wales.[86] The Cornwallis and Southwell families were linked through marriage.[87]

Cornwallis's ownership is confirmed by other evidence. He stated in 1624, in a case brought by Gonville and Caius College concerning their Windhams manor in Burnham Thorpe, that he had bought 'divers other lands and tenements sometimes Robert Jennysons and one Bostons and of the scyte of the late dissolved priory of Fryers Carmelites in Burnham Norton with the appurtenances'.[88] Jenyson's lands were probably those of the 1566 conveyance, Bostons' lands may refer to Vyncentes Close, but the vendor of the Friary site is unidentified: maybe it was Cobbe.

Phase XV. Sturges (Friary site & lands?)

The next owner of the property was Thomas Sturges, although his ownership could have been only brief, as his name is absent from Spelman's list.[89] Nevertheless, the transfer of the Friary from Cornwallis to Sturges is stated in the 1624 Gonville and Caius College case mentioned above,[90] and is confirmed by an eighteenth-century copy of a conveyance of 1616/17.[91] Very little detail is available, owing to the document's fragility and poor condition, except that the conveyance was from 'Charles Cornewallys', George Towneshend, Leonard Mayes, Jonas Pytt and Ralph Laughton to Thomas Sturges (or Sturgis), possibly of Thetford (Norfolk).[92]

Phase XVI. Soame (Friary site & lands?)

Cornwallis' testimony of 1624 reveals that the Friary was assured to Thomas and John Soame, but how this fact relates to the transfer to

---

[85] Blomefield & Parkin, *History of Norfolk*, vol. VII, pp.9, 35; Caius, *Annals of Gonville and Caius*, p.316.

[86] *ODNB*, 'Cornwallis, Sir Charles (*c.*1555–1629)'.

[87] Rye, *Visitacion of Norfolk*, p.260; Marshall, *Visitations of Nottingham*, p.162.

[88] Caius, *Annals of Gonville and Caius*, p.316.

[89] Spelman, *History of Sacrilege*, p.252.

[90] Caius, *Annals of Gonville and Caius*, p.316.

[91] CRO F/4/177/9.

[92] CRO pers. comm., 22 November 2018.

Sturges is unclear unless the estate was fragmented again, or Sturges himself transferred it straight to the Soames.[93] According to Spelman, one 'Alderman Soame' bought the Friary from Cornwallis.[94] This figure is most probably Sir Stephen Soame (c.1544–1619), Lord Mayor of London, purchaser of Burnham Deepdale manor in 1598,[95] Polstead Hall manor (from Cornwallis) in 1616,[96] and father to Thomas and John.[97] Sir Stephen died a very rich man, having enough property, in six counties including Norfolk, to provide his four surviving sons with landed estates.[98]

The site next passed to John Soame, second son of Alderman Soame,[99] and the last name in Spelman's list (written c.1623). John Soame was also lord of Burnham Deepdale manor in 1656.[100] He could be the 'advena' (outsider) buried at Burnham Thorpe in 1663/4. It is assumed the site passed to his son, John junior, who died in 1673. The young John was 'a very hopefull man; he was a very good scholler, and a fine well-qualified gentleman; died when marriageable; a great loss to, may I say ruine of, their familie,' lamented a relative.[101]

Phase XVII. Palmer (Friary site & lands?)

We now depart from Spelman's list and return to archival sources of evidence. John Soame junior's nuncupative will (i.e. a will declared orally) of 20 November 1673 (proved 13 December) named his maternal grandfather, and guardian, Sir William Palmer (d. 1682) as the sole executor, stating that Palmer 'shall enjoy all my Estate' including, presumably, his Friary property.[102] The will also made provision for two of Soame's cousins (Mary Garney and John Bramstone). The following year, the ecclesiastical court upheld the will, and in its

---

93 Caius, *Annals of Gonville and Caius*, p.316.
94 Spelman, *History of Sacrilege*, p.252.
95 Bryant, *Churches of Norfolk*, p.10.
96 Blomefield & Parkin *History of Norfolk*, vol. VII, pp.10, 35.
97 Caius, *Annals of Gonville and Caius*, pp.316–17.
98 Mimardière, 'Soame, Sir Stephen (c.1544–1619)'.
99 Spelman, *History of Sacrilege*, p.252.
100 Blomefield & Parkin, *History of Norfolk*, vol. VII, p.10.
101 Bramston, *Autobiography*, p.24; Blomefield & Parkin, *History of Norfolk*, vol. VII, p.11.
102 TNA PROB 11/343/488; Bramston, *Autobiography*, p.24.

sentence mentioned other cousins of Soame: Anna Harris the wife of John Harris, as well as Hugh, Simon, Sarah, Hannah and Anna Middleton,[103] some of whom we shall meet below.

Phase XVIII. Savile and Myddleton (Friary site & lands?)

The Friary site and/or lands had been united with Polstead Hall and Burnham Lexhams manors and four local church advowsons as one bloc of property by 1675.[104] Then, it was all in the hands of Thomas Savile, Esq. and Hugh Myddleton, Gent. The two men seem to have been related, but the evidence is complex and contradictory. Some sources imply Savile (probably of Lupset Hall, Wakefield, Yorkshire) and Myddleton were cousins, and the likely co-heirs of the Soame estates through their mothers, the daughters of John Soame senior (Myddleton's parents were Simon Myddleton and his second wife, Mary Soame, one of John Soame senior's daughters).[105] In addition, Myddleton's sister Mary married Edmund Soame, one of John Soame senior's nephews. However, another source states that all of John Soame senior's offspring died without issue.[106] It seems likely that Palmer disposed of the Friary to Savile and Myddleton shortly after John Soame junior's death.

Phase XIX. Tyndall (Friary site & manor)

In 1675, Savile and Myddleton sold the above manors and advowsons to one Thomas Tyndall for £2,000.[107] The Friary premises was described as the 'Manor of the late dissolved Carmelite Priory otherwise Burnham Norton, otherwise Nortons, and the site of the Priory'. The various manors in this sale comprised land in Burnhams Deepdale, Norton, Overy, St Andrew's, Sutton, Ulph, and Westgate, but the locations, acreages and names of the lands were unrecorded.

---

[103] TNA PROB 11/346/14.

[104] NRO WAL 820, 281X5.

[105] Anon., *English Baronetage*, vol. III(II), p.697; Greenwood, *Ecclesiastical History of Dewsbury*, pp.211–12; Banks, *Walks in Yorkshire*, p.134. This Hugh Myddleton was the grandson of Sir Hugh Myddleton, who constructed the New River to convey water from springs near Ware (Hertfordshire) into London.

[106] Burke & Burke, *Extinct and Dormant Baronetcies*, pp.496–7.

[107] NRO WAL 820, 281X5.

Phase XX. Myddleton and Soame (Friary messuage, tenement & farm)

In 1689, Sir Hugh 'Middleton' (Myddleton), late of Hackney in Middlesex, and Bartholomew Soame, goldsmith of London, still retained property connected to the Friary.[108] Bartholomew Soame may have been another nephew of John Soame senior of Burnham Westgate.[109]

Myddleton and Bartholomew Soame's Friary holding comprised:

i. The 'Messuage Tenement and Farme of the late dissolved house or priory of the Order of the Carmelites' with arable lands, sheep feedings, fold courses, saltmarshes and a 4-acre piece of fresh marsh, in Burnhams Norton and St Andrew. It had formerly been in the tenure of Edmund Lyme, then Clement Woodrow, and it was a parcel of the demesne of the Friary.

ii. 30 acres of arable lands in Burnham Sutton in the common fields and 4 acres of enclosed land in the same parish (tenant: Widow Harris).

iii. A 2-acre parcel of meadow called Roydons, in Burnham Overy (tenant: ditto).

The messuage, farm and lands were called 'Fryers Farme', formerly 'Norton Farme', and their annual value was £105.[110] The use of the word 'demesne' in the case of another Carmelite friary has been interpreted as meaning part of the walled precinct.[111] This phase in the Friary's history may record a further fragmentation of the Friary estate.

Phase XXI. Goldsmith and Appleford (Friary messuage, tenement & farm)

In April 1689, 'Sir Hugh Midleton's Estate Act' was passed in Parliament. It confirmed a settlement for the separate maintenance of his wife Dorothea and daughter Dorothy, and other trusts, and the sale of part of his estate to pay his debts. On 25 May, Myddleton and Bartholomew Soame vested the Friary messuage, tenement and farm in John Goldsmith of the Middle Temple and

---

[108] NRO WAL 876/1, 282X4.
[109] Howard, *Visitation of London*, p.251.
[110] NRO WAL 876/1, 282X4.
[111] At Hulne (O'Sullivan, *In the Company of Preachers*, p.168).

William Appleford of Westminster in Middlesex,[112] presumably Dame Dorothea's trustees.

Phase XXII. Smith (Friary messuage, tenement & farm)

Goldsmith and Appleford sold the messuage, tenement and farm on 17 May 1690 to John Smith of Thistleworth (Isleworth) in Middlesex for £1,700. Smith, son of an alderman of the City of London, was created Baronet Smith of Isleworth in 1694 after having 'advanced several sums of money towards carrying on the war with France'. He became one of the gentlemen of the privy chamber of King William and, later, Queen Anne, and he died in 1726.[113]

In 1690, the land was identical to the 1689 description, the only difference being that the former tenant was listed as Edmund Lynne not Lyme as above.

In *c*.1720, the estate was called 'Friery Farme' and was occupied by Bacon Hibgame of Burnham Norton. The relationship between Hibgame and his fellow villagers had turned sour because of a quarrel over grazing rights of the farm's flock (which was up to 400-head strong) on the Common Marsh near the farm. Smith and Hibgame claimed that:

> ... there hath antiently beene for time out of minde of man and still is a Custom for the tennant or occupyer of the said Farme in every year from Lady Day to Michaelmas to turn in and feed and Depasture his flock of Sheep in and over the said Common Marsh And from Michaelmas to Lady Day to turn in and Feed and Depasture his said flock of Sheep in and over all the Infold Land in the Common field of Burnham Norton.[114]

The villagers explained that the use of the Common Marsh was not by right but by the consent of the commoners, in return for a suitable recompense, an arrangement that went back around 40 years. The details of the case date the existence of a flock at 'Friery Farme' back to at least *c*.1680, the beginning of Smith's ownership to *c*.1706 (sixteen years later than his apparent purchase of the property), and the start of Hibgame's tenancy to *c*.1709.

[112] NRO WAL 876/1, 282X4.
[113] Burke & Burke, *Extinct and Dormant Baronetcies*, p.494.
[114] TNA C11/2666/32.

XXIII. Weddell in trust for Harris (Friary manor)

The next mention of the Friary is in a trust deed of 1700 which conveyed the Friary manor, as well as Polstead Hall and Burnham Lexhams manors, and various church advowsons in the Burnhams, to one John Weddell (probably the family lawyer)[115] to give use to John Harris (junior) and thereafter his heirs.[116] John Harris senior, lord of Polstead Hall manor and of Burnham Deepdale manor (the latter in 1686),[117] was Savile's brother-in-law (see Phase *XVIII*), from whom he had inherited Lupset Hall. John Harris senior died in 1691/2[118] (meaning the 'Widow Harris' mentioned under Phase *XX* in 1689 could not have been his widow) and the younger John sold Lupset Hall in 1699.[119]

The Friary premises was simply listed as the 'Manor of the late dissolved house or priory of the Order of the Carmelites with the Rights members and appurtenances thereof in Burnham Norton and elsewhere in Norfolk.'

Phase XXIV. Lombard (Friary messuage, tenement & farm)

Sir John Smith, his wife Dame Mary, son John Smith Esq. and one Richarde Bourchier sold the premises in 1723 to Peter Lombard of Burnham Thorpe for £1,700.[120] Lombard, formerly of St Martin-in-the-Fields, London, was a fascinating figure: a Huguenot refugee, once the *Faiseur des corsets* of Queen Marie Thérèse[121] (wife of Louis XIV of France), and later described as 'sometime diamond merchant of London and purveyor to Queen Anne'.[122] Lombard seems to have begun acquiring land in the local area by about 1707.[123] He went on

---

[115] John Weddell (of Lincoln's Inn), was involved in many property conveyances made by the Harrises (Taylor, *History of Wakefield*, pp.132–4). Advowson: the right to present a clergyman to a benefice.

[116] WYAS KM/852; Sheila Sweetinburgh pers. comm., 15 October 2020.

[117] Bryant, *Churches of Norfolk*, p.10.

[118] Wentworth, *Complete System of Pleading*, vol. X, p.96; TNA PROB 11/409/175.

[119] Greenwood, *Ecclesiastical History of Dewsbury*, pp.211–12; Banks, *Walks in Yorkshire*, p.134.

[120] NRO WAL 876/5, 282X4.

[121] Bryant, *Churches of Norfolk*, p.24.

[122] Baxter, *England's Rise to Greatness*, p.274.

[123] E.g. NRO WAL 900, 283X1. Maybe Smith and Lombard met at the court of Queen Anne.

to hold several local manors: Burnham Thorpe, Burnham Vewters, Pomfretts and Hall Close.

Lombard's purchase consisted of the messuage, tenement and farm of the dissolved house of Carmelites, described in almost the same way as in 1689, except that it now had three different tenants: Clement Woodrow, Widow Harris, and John Hibgame (who held the sheepwalk and sheepcourse of 'Fryers Farm'). Plans were afoot after the 1723 sale for the embanking or 'taking in of the marshes', by which the 'Fryers Estate ... may be so improved to a considerable advantage'.[124]

Phase XXV. Walpole (later Earls of Orford, Wolterton estate) (Friary messuage, tenement & farm)

Lombard died in 1725. That portion of the Lombard estates including the Friary passed into the Walpole family of Wolterton as a result of the 1720 marriage of Lombard's daughter and co-heir Mary Magdalen to Horatio Walpole (1678–1757).[125] Through this union, Walpole 'obtained a considerable fortune', allowing him to buy and rebuild Wolterton Hall, the family's principal home, and purchase Mannington Hall (both in Norfolk).[126] After a long career in politics and diplomacy (including fighting a duel in the House of Commons), he was created 1st Baron Walpole of Wolterton in 1756.[127]

The Friary estate's descent through the Walpole family involved five generations, all MPs, four of whom had the same name. In 1757, it passed to the 1st Baron's son, also Horatio (1723–1809; the 2nd Baron). This man was created Earl of Orford (of the third creation) in 1806.[128] The Friary was inherited by his son, another Horatio (1752–1822;

---

[124] NRO MC 567/1–22, 778X4. Letter, 1723–4, from Robert Discipline to Peter Lombard.

[125] Coxe, *Memoirs of Horatio Lord Walpole*, pp.463–4; Warburton, *Memoirs of Horace Walpole*, vol. II, p.575; NRO WAL 1162, 282X6. Horatio Walpole was a younger brother of Sir Robert Walpole of Houghton (Norfolk), the country's first prime minister.

[126] Coxe, *Memoirs of Horatio Lord Walpole*, pp.463–4.

[127] Sedgwick, 'Walpole, Horatio (1678–1757)'.

[128] Sedgwick, 'Walpole, Hon. Horatio (1723–1809)'. He also inherited the title Baron Walpole of Walpole from his uncle in 1797, but to avoid confusion, this title is not listed in the brief biographies of the Walpoles here. The Earl's son was given the courtesy title, Lord Walpole.

the 2nd Earl and 3rd Baron).[129] Next it came his son, also Horatio (1783–1858; the 3rd Earl and 4th Baron). He had diplomatic roles in Madrid and St Petersburg. This 'diminutive, anti-Catholic figure' was also described as an 'inveterate gambler, anti-feminist and 'poseur', neglectful of his wife'.[130] He and his son, Horatio William (1813–1894; the 4th Earl and 5th Baron) would go on to dramatically alter the physical remains of the Friary (see Chapter 3). Horatio William made Mannington his main home. He was a Catholic convert,[131] and a wife-beater.[132] With no sons from his short-lived marriage, Horatio William was succeeded by his nephew, Robert Horace (1854–1931; the 5th Earl and 6th Baron), the last Walpole to own the Friary site.

How did the Friary estate fare under the Walpoles? The lands' descriptions and the tenants in 1725 were identical to those of 1723.[133] A 1753 lease of 'Friary Farm', on behalf of Horatio Walpole, lists houses, barns and stables at the site, and reveals the holding had grown to include tenements recently bought from John Bensley and John Bennington.[134] The out-going tenant was Catherine Hibgame, and the farm was taken on by Thomas Foley. Amongst Foley's many duties was a requirement to sow 15 acres of turnips on the 'inclosed lands' and the same amount 'in the common field'. The summer leys had to be 'teathed'[135] with the

[129] Drummond, 'Walpole, Hon. Horatio (1752–1822)'.

[130] Healey & Escott, 'Walpole, Horatio, Lord Walpole (1783–1858)'.

[131] Healey & Escott, 'Walpole, Horatio, Lord Walpole (1783–1858)'.

[132] Rintoul, *Dictionary of Real People and Places in Fiction*, p.926.

[133] NRO WAL 1162, 282X6.

[134] NRO WLP 8/33, 1044X8. John Bensley's tenement comprised a barn, stable, outhouses and gardens, a 5-rood pightle and 11 parcels of land totalling 13 acres in the field of Burnham Norton (NRO WAL 1083, 285X3). Their location is unknown. John Bennington's tenement included houses, malthouses and barns, a premises called the Homestall, and 24 parcels of land totalling 19 acres & 3 roods (NRO WAL 119/1, 269X5).

[135] 'Teathe' (noun and verb) (alternatively, 'tathe'): the dialect word for the beneficial effect of folding (temporarily fencing and grazing) livestock on arable land. It was a term that conveyed more than just the benefit of the animal's manure on the soil: the positive effects of their urine, trampling hooves, perspiration, breath and warmth were also thought important (Marshall, *Rural Economy of Norfolk*, vol. I, pp.33–4). The 'teathe' on light land was 'one of the main supports of the Norfolk system of husbandry' (*ibid.*, p.361).

farm's whole flock of sheep, Foley had to find straw for thatching, and also 'Imbarn and stack all the Corn from the premises'.

Later, the *c.*1840 Burnham Norton parish tithe map[136] reveals that the Friary precinct's (and farmstead's) occupiers were the executors of the late William Mack (d. 1838), who had also been the tenant of the village's principal holding, Norton Hall Farm, Walpole property too. Mack's executors occupied so much land in Burnham Norton that it is impossible to use the tithe map to make any conclusions about which pieces may have belonged to 'Friary Farm.'

On 9 October 1843, the live- and deadstock of John Savory, a later tenant of 'Friar's Farm' in Burnham Norton, was auctioned because he was relinquishing the premises:

> Livestock consists of: 120 half-bred shearlings fit for the butcher, 20 half-bred shearling ewes, 15 half-bred stock ewes, 170 capital half-bred Down & Leicester lambs, 5 fat short-horn steers, 9 short-horns forward in condition, red Norfolk cow & calf, handsome 3-yr-old roan Durham bull, 3 useful young carthorses and mares, black nag mare 5-yrs-old, a quantity of poultry.
>
> Ag. carriages etc.: 4 horse-power threshing machine, in good condition, road wagon, muck tumbrel, water cart, luggage cart, two-horse jointed iron roll, trace barley roll, 4 bullock bins, 13 covered and open sheep troughs, set of cart harness, hand chaff box & knife, 2 wagon wheels, 2 corn bins, turnip slicer, forks, rakes, ladders etc.[137]

Threshing machines were becoming common on large farms in the 1840s.[138] The significance of such machinery, with respect to the Friary's physical remains, is detailed in Section 3.6. Friar's Farm must have had implement sheds, stabling and maybe cattle yards, as well as both arable and pasture land. The sale notice is the last known document to mention Friar's Farm.

Much later, in 1917 and by then under the ownership of the 5th Earl, the Friary precinct underwent a brief period as a prisoners-of-war camp (see Appendix 2).

---

[136] NRO DN/TA 229.
[137] *Norfolk Chronicle* 16 September 1843, p.4.
[138] Susanna Wade-Martins pers. comm., 4 November 2020.

Phase XXVI. Coke (Earls of Leicester, Holkham estate) (Friary site &
precinct, with other lands)

The Walpoles owned the Friary for almost two centuries; however, in 1922 the site, along with the rest of their holdings in Burnham Norton and nearby, was bought by Thomas William Coke, 3rd Earl of Leicester, from the 5th Earl of Orford.[139] Friary Cottage was divided from the rest of the former Friary and sold into separate ownership in 1968, with the Cokes retaining the remainder of the site. The precinct was one of the grazing marshes of Mill Farm, Burnham Overy Staithe, until 2000.[140] In 2010, the ruins and precinct (excluding Friary Cottage) were leased to the Norfolk Archaeological Trust for a term of 50 years.

2.4 TOPONYMIC EVIDENCE OF THE FRIARY ESTATE

As well as the archival and published sources examined above, the Friary estate has been further investigated by studying local toponyms (place-names and field-names), which were recorded by the present author from cartographical and oral history sources.[141] No extant or historical (dating from *c.*1796 onwards in the above study) place-names contained the terms 'Whitefriars', 'Carmelites' or their derivatives in the Burnhams, though it is clear from pre-Dissolution wills that the term 'Whitefriars' was in use by local people.[142] In addition to the term 'Friars Lane', the word 'Friary' or 'Friars' occurs in four other local toponyms at the Friary site or abutting it (Fig. 3). Two of the four toponymns appear to only date from 1840: in 1825/6, the friary precinct was called 'Walled Yard', and the site of 'Lower Friars Field' was covered by 'Primrose Pightell' and 'Overy Field'. Aside from the precinct itself, which is known former Carmelite property, whether or not the other pieces of land were once held by the Friary, or simply named to reflect their proximity to it, is unknown.

139 Holkham Hall Archives, 'Conveyance between the Earl of Orford and the Earl of Leicester. 8 June 1922'.
140 Holly Smith pers. comm., 21 January 2021.
141 Francis, *Clarky Bottoms and Small Hopes.*
142 E.g. Nicholas Goldale's will of 1514 (Alban, 'Benefactors Great and Small', pp.162–3).

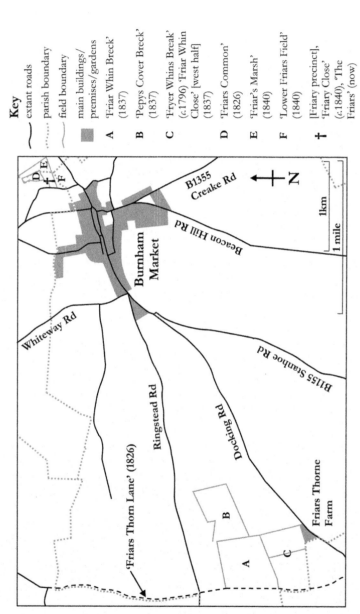

Key

— extant roads
···· parish boundary
⌒ field boundary
▦ main buildings/premises/gardens

A 'Friar Whin Breck' (1837)

B 'Pepys Cover Breck' (1837)

C 'Fryer Whins Break' (*c.*1796) 'Friar Whin Close' [west half] (1837)

D 'Triars Common' (1826)

E 'Friar's Marsh' (1840)

F 'Lower Friars Field' (1840)

† [Friary precinct], 'Friary Close' (*c.*1840), 'The Friars' (now)

Figure 3. Local toponyms containing the elements 'Friary' or 'Friars'. © The author.

A more intriguing toponym is in the westernmost part of Burnham Westgate, abutting the parish boundary and well away from the Friary itself: 'Friars Thorne Farm', alternatively called Friar's Thorn, or Friar Thorn, and formerly, Friars Whin.[143] No buildings appear at the site on a c.1796 survey of Polstead Hall and Burnham Lexhams manors (the oldest known detailed map of this area)[144] nor on the parish tithe map of 1837, and Friars Thorne Farm house only bears the date 1847.[145] However, variants of the toponym occurred to the north-west of the current farm in field-names, although their historical boundaries do not exactly correspond with the modern ones. The two fields immediately north of the current farm were called 'Fryer Whins Break', or 'Fryer Whins Corner', c.1796. The western part was renamed 'Friar Whin Close' by 1837, but now that name is forgotten, and the field is simply called 'The Thirty-seven Acres'.[146] North of this was 'Friar Whin Breck' (1837) now part of a larger field called 'Fourscore'. The minor road west of the farm, and bordering this field, was called 'Friars Thorn Lane' in 1826.[147] Remembering that the Pepys family were formerly involved in the ownership of the Friary, it may be significant that 'Papers Breck',[148] near Friars Thorne Farm, was 'Pepys Cover Breck' in 1837. In c.1796, this was part of a larger field extending eastwards: 'Pepys Breck'.

The history of Friars Thorne in Burnham Westgate is poorly understood. A local amateur historian thought it might relate to a chapel of ease for pilgrims, administered by the Carmelites,[149] but no such chapel is mentioned by the antiquarian Blomefield or other writers, nor is it in the Norfolk Historic Environment Record. By contrast, the similar toponyms, Great and Little Friar's Thorne (earlier called Priors-Thorns) near Swaffham (Norfolk) are named for the site of a former pilgrims' hostel run between 1154 and 1537 by the Cistercian monks of Sawtrey Abbey (Huntingdonshire).[150]

---

143 Francis, *Clarky Bottoms and Small Hopes*, Plates 9 & 13. 'Whin': the Norfolk dialect word for gorse, a plant indicating poor quality, sandy soil.
144 NRO MC 1830/1, 852X7.
145 Francis pers. ob.
146 Francis, *Clarky Bottoms and Small Hopes*, Plate 13.
147 Barringer, *Bryant's Map of Norfolk*, p.6.
148 Francis, *Clarky Bottoms and Small Hopes*, Plate 13.
149 The late Bridget Everitt pers. comm., 2007.
150 Blomefield & Parkin, *History of Norfolk*, vol. VI, p.205; NHER 3977.

2.5 DISCUSSION

The post-Dissolution ownership history of Burnham Norton Friary is long and convoluted. During the 480 years after the Carmelites left, the Friary changed hands many times. It descended through complex lineages in extended families and the estate was also fragmented, making its story all the more difficult to unravel. Based on the available evidence, what is believed to be a near-complete sequence of owners has now been compiled; they range from courtiers living outside the county, to more modest status (though still 'gentry' class) individuals from the Burnhams. By gaining a better understanding of the Friary's ownership history, we learn important new detail about the Friary buildings, the Friary estate and the farmstead which developed on the site. This descent of property also helps illuminate, and gives substance to, the wider changes in the patterns of land ownership of which it was part.

The first person to express an interest in the Friary, before it was even dissolved, was Lady Jane Calthorpe. She had personal reasons for wanting to acquire a property in the Burnhams, but her thinking may have been influenced by other factors too. The Calthorpes were closely linked with the Carmelite Order in Norfolk. A member of the family had been a Carmelite friar at Norwich in 1426. Additionally, Sir William, grandfather of the elder Sir Philip, was buried in the Norwich Carmelites' church in 1494, alongside his first wife and four of his children.[151] Another relative, John Calthorp [*sic*] claimed founder status at Blakeney Friary,[152] also a Carmelite house. Lady Jane would have been aware of the 'ancient custom' that it was lawful for the families of founders[153] to 'resume all lands bestowed for charitable and religious uses, if they were not applied to the purposes for which they were given.'[154] She may also have had 'curatorial concerns' for any Calthorpe tombs inside Burnham Norton

---

[151] Carr-Calthrop, *Families of Calthorpe and Calthrop*, pp.42, 44.

[152] O'Sullivan, *In the Company of Preachers*, p.26.

[153] The role of founder was heritable (O'Sullivan, *In the Company of Preachers*, p.12).

[154] Blunt, *Reformation of the Church of England*, p.376. The dissolved Ludlow Carmelite Friary was first leased to a person claiming founders' rights (O'Sullivan, *In the Company of Preachers*, p.235).

Friary church.[155] She would additionally have been mindful that her late husband's relatives leased part of a mansion at Blakeney Friary in 1537.[156]

Although it appears that Lady Jane may not have obtained the Friary in 1538, she was the tenant of significant parts of it earlier than previously thought, possibly in 1539. By May 1541, she was tenant of the claustral buildings and a stable opposite the gatehouse. The presence of this stable may explain the unidentified parchmark, now covered by the site of Burnham Market Primary School, in a 1951 aerial photograph.[157] It has long been thought that the Friary's activities may have been on both sides of Friars Lane, and evidence of the stable lends weight to that idea. The stable stood on 1 rood of pasture. It may be mere coincidence, but it is possible this could be the 1 rood of 'meadow' given to the friars in 1298, land that has previously been interpreted as being adjacent to the precinct.[158]

Lady Jane also occupied a house on a 3-acre plot, associated with the Friary but with an imprecisely-described location in the archival sources, and not mentioned in the Ministers' and Receivers' Accounts. The east portion of the Friary precinct, defined by a small terrace on the 5m contour, has been measured at approximately 3 acres,[159] and here, magnetometry surveying in 2017 revealed the buried remains of a significant but previously unknown building, putatively identified as a gatehouse (see Fig. 2).[160] It is interesting to speculate whether instead, these are the remains of the house on the 3-acre plot, and if so, whether Lady Jane lived in it. If this was the case, it suggests a building of suitable status for a woman who had once figured highly in court life. The presence of a founder's (or other layperson's) house or mansion

---

[155] O'Sullivan, *In the Company of Preachers*, p.26. The brass to John Calthorp (d. 1503) of Cockthorpe, Norfolk (seat of the so-called senior branch of the junior Calthorpe line) was relocated from Blakeney Friary to the parish church presumably by his descendants at the Dissolution.

[156] Wright, 'Blakeney Carmelite Friary', p.13.

[157] Emery, 'Archaeological Surveys of the Burnham Norton Site', p.72.

[158] Chester-Kadwell, 'Site at Burnham Norton and its Landscape Context', p.60.

[159] Chester-Kadwell, 'Site at Burnham Norton and its Landscape Context', pp.60–1.

[160] Bescoby, 'Imagined Land', p.10; Emery, 'Archaeological Surveys of the Burnham Norton Site', pp.74–5.

within a friary precinct is not unknown, as already mentioned in the case of Blakeney. Other Carmelite examples include the 'founder's lodging' at Gloucester, the tower at Hulne, and a tenement inside the 'bailey' (precinct) at Marlborough.[161] There is no mention in the archives of the house on the 3 acres being new, so maybe it was built before the Dissolution. It could well have been rented out in 1535, a period when many religious houses leased parts of their precincts, although it is not itemised separately in the *Valor*'s brief entry for the Friary. It may have initially been included under the general heading of the 'site and house' of the former Friary in 1539. There is no information about the house on the 3-acre plot after 1561.

We now turn to wider aspects of the Friary estate, beginning with an attempt to reconcile the pre-Dissolution 68-acre extent listed by the *Valor*, with the information found in the later archival sources. The present author has worked through many hypothetical scenarios using the data from this study and will present the most parsimonious option. We shall begin with the assumption that the 3 acres with the house on it was part of the friars' 68-acre income-generating estate even though it was within their precinct. The rest of their precinct, if not rented out, would not have featured in the *Valor*. This means the real acreage controlled by the friars was probably 68 acres plus that part of their precinct outside the 3 acres portion, say *c.*70 acres in all.

By the time the Friary was dissolved, 20 acres of its original estate had been granted away clandestinely on long leases by the friars as concealed lands, probably to their friends in the local community.[162] This land was only recovered by the Crown decades later (Phases *XI, XII* & *XIII*). Grants such as these occurred all over the country in the years up to the Dissolution, and any made after 1536 were treated as being illegal by the Crown.[163] The motives of the friars may have been that, foreseeing the Friary's imminent demise, they tried to confound the efforts of the commissioners to seize their property for the Crown. Maybe there was a hope that one day they might be able to re-establish their community so they therefore wanted to place their land in safekeeping. However, they may have been pushed into making their grants to raise funds urgently because from winter

---

[161] O'Sullivan, *In the Company of Preachers*, pp.145, 166, 238.
[162] Clark, *Dissolution of the Monasteries*, p.305.
[163] Clark, *Dissolution of the Monasteries*, p.464.

1537, all friaries' incomes 'melted away' as lay people stopped giving them alms.[164] Concealed lands were pursued by commissioners during the reigns of Edward VI, Mary and Elizabeth and warrants for the various inquisitions were eagerly sought by courtiers.[165]

Given the strong links between the Carmelites and the Calthorpes, it seems likely that this family could have been the recipients of the Friary's concealed lands. The loss of these 20 acres meant that only 48 acres was at the disposal of the Dissolution commissioners in 1538. When the Crown granted the Friary site and lands to Cobham and Warner in 1541, the lands' area was further reduced to 39 acres & 3⅓ roods plus the unmeasured 'house and site' of the Friary. It follows therefore that 48 acres minus 39 acres & 3⅓ roods, in other words 8 acres & ⅔ rood, had vanished from the written records. Where did this land go?

The answer may be deduced after comparing the creditors' payments before and after the Dissolution (see Table 2), which reveals much interesting information. Some payments remained the same. There was no change to those to Southwell, Pomfretts manor and the parish church, implying these were not remittances for food or fuel for the friars (who were now of course absent), but were rents for lands. That the payments were identical shows that Cobham and Warner and their successors carried on using Southwell's, Pomfretts manor's and the parish church's land as part of the post-Dissolution Friary estate. The same is probably true of the rented lands belonging to Fyncham at Deepdale manor. Although there was a penny decrease in that manor's dues, this is possibly an accounting error.

Sir Philip Calthorpe's payment reduced drastically after the Dissolution. This might be because some of the lands he inherited in 1535 from his father, Sir Philip senior, were redistributed to Lady Jane and their kinswoman Elizabeth after the Calthorpe legal dispute of c.1537 (see Phase I, above), making the two women into new creditors. However, the post-Dissolution dues collected by all three Calthorpes totalled only 4s. 7d., which means that Calthorpe lands worth 3s. 4d. in 1535 were no longer part of the Friary estate by 1539–41. These observations suggest that the 'missing' 8 acres & ⅔ rood described above,

---

[164] Clark, *Dissolution of the Monasteries*, p.352. For the same reason, friars throughout the country were forced into selling their communities' household goods to survive.

[165] Clark, *Dissolution of the Monasteries*, pp.304, 542.

Table 2. Comparison of creditors' payments from the Friary's
pre- and post-Dissolution phases. Shaded areas indicate
payments that remained unchanged. As shown in the 1566
schedule, but not appreciated before its analysis, Pomfretts
manor had land in Burnhams Norton and Westgate, and
Hall Close manor had land in Burnham Norton.

Creditor	Pre-Dissolution (1535)	Post-Dissolution (1539–41)
Philip Calthorp(e) (manor of Burnham Thorpe)	7s. 11d.	15d. (= 1s. 3d.)
Richard Southwell, Lexhams manor	2s. 7d.	2s. 7d.
College of Pountfrett/ Pomfrete (Pomfretts manor)	7½d.	7½d.
Walsingham Priory	12d.	Dissolved, presumably the dues included in the rest of the payment to the Crown if the ex-Walsingham land was still included in the Friary estate
John Fyncham(e) (Deepdale)	19d.	18d.
Church/Rectory of Burnham Norton	8d.	8d.
House of St John at Carbrooke	1d. (maybe only a donation)	Dissolved, no dues paid or donation made
Hugh Thurlowe	2d.	No dues paid, though Thurlowe was still alive at this date
Jane Calthorpe, Polstead Hall manor	–	2s. 6d.
'Elysabeth Calthorpe', Hall Close manor	–	10d.
Totals	14s. 7½d.	9s. 11½d.

was taken back by the Calthorpes when the Friary was dissolved. They might have installed new tenants on this land (possibly John Pepys, Philip Calthorpe's tenant in 1539),[166] farmed it in-hand, or sold it. In any case it did not pass to Cobham and Warner. It would have added to the Calthorpes' concealed lands, making their portion of the old Friary estate 28 acres & ⅔ rood in extent.

Delving further into the Calthorpes' figures, their reduction in payment represents one third of all the creditors' total in 1539–1541. This suggests that three-quarters of those lands that the Carmelites once rented from local landlords were probably transferred to Cobham and Warner, whilst the remaining one quarter returned to the Calthorpes. Assuming that this quarter share is represented by the 8 acres & ⅔ rood identified above, and that all the lands were let at the same rate per acre by the various landlords, then the original extent of lands rented by the Carmelites in 1535 was four times 8 acres & ⅔ rood. This equals 32 acres & 2⅔ roods. Building on this calculation, 35 acres & 1⅓ roods (the remainder of the 68 acres) seems to have been the lands originally endowed to the Carmelites.

Some payments were extinguished after the Dissolution. First, Walsingham Priory's payment disappeared because the Priory was dissolved (in 1538). Assuming the Priory's land continued to be used by the tenants of the Friary estate, its dues would have been paid to the Crown and not separately itemised in the post-Dissolution list of creditors. Second, Hugh Thurlowe's payment of 2d. may have been for food or fuel rather than a rent since he was still alive when the post-Dissolution creditors list was drawn up, yet was no longer being paid. The Carbrooke Preceptory's tiny payment in 1535 may have been a donation rather than a rent as discussed earlier.

In 1566, Jenyson bought property from Bromefelde/Bromfield and Pepes/Pepys: Vyncentes Close and a further 58 acres & ¼ rood (58.0625 acres) of arable lands still identified 28 years after the Dissolution as formerly being the friars' (Phase *VIII*). This total area is much larger than the 39 acres & 3⅓ roods plus 'house and site' of the Friary that Bromfield and Pepys bought in 1561 (Phase *VII*). The only explanation for this huge discrepancy is that they somehow acquired the Calthorpes' lands above to expand their holding. This might have been via John Pepys. Perhaps some years after the Dissolution, with there being no

[166] *L&P Hen. VIII*, vol. XIV(I), p.556.

prospect of the Friary being re-established, the Calthorpes sold off their concealed and other lands connected with the Friary.

Before they broke it up, Bromfield and Pepys' Friary holding comprised the unmeasured 'house and site', the house on 3 acres, the 1 rood with the stable, Le Asshe Pightell, Vyncentes Close, and the endowed and rented lands formerly the Carmelites' out in the fields. Adding all these properties' areas together gives 65 acres & 3¼ roods. Remarkably, Bromfield and Pepys had almost reassembled the pre-Dissolution estate, but some land is missing. To make up the shortfall, we must turn to the concealed marshes, 2 acres, that were once in John Wightman's occupation (Phase *XI*). Wightman has no known connection to the Friary which might have led to his being granted these 2 acres by the Carmelites, so instead it is likely he obtained it from the Calthorpes. Bromfield and Pepys' Friary holding at its maximum size, plus Wightman's marshes totals 67 acres & 3¼ roods (67.8125 acres), a very close approximation to the *Valor*'s 68 acres.

Jenyson enjoyed the use of all his Friary property until the commissioners caught up with him in 1575 and recovered 16 acres of concealed lands (Phase *XII*). At an unknown date, Bromfield and Pepys (or their successors) sold the Friary 'house and site', the house on 3 acres, the 1 rood with the stable, and Le Asshe Pightell to an unknown buyer, possibly Southwell. It is interesting that Southwell, given his knowledge of the Friary as a creditor, a neighbouring landowner and a commissioner, did not seek to acquire the site much earlier than he did. Maybe in 1538 he was busy chasing bigger prizes. Southwell later presumably sold the Friary 'house and site' etc. to Cobbe (Phase *X*). In 1576, 2 acres of concealed ex-Friary land was confiscated from Cobbe (Phase *XIII*). This cannot have been included within the 'house and site', the house on 3 acres, the 1 rood with the stable, and Le Asshe Pightell, or be Vyncentes Close, because all those items had been known to the Crown for years. It is probable therefore that Jenyson sold Cobbe, his relative, this 2 acres at some date before his remaining concealed 16 acres was taken away. As a final observation about the concealed lands, their locations show that the friars' endowed lands lay in Burnhams Deepdale, Norton, St Andrew's and Westgate. Before this analysis of the 1566 conveyance and the concealed lands, it was not clear that the Friary estate extended into Burnhams Deepdale and St Andrew's.

Later, it is likely that Cornwallis purchased Cobbe's and Jenyson's reduced acreages of Friary lands. This allowed Cornwallis to partially reconstruct the Friary estate once again, but this time without the 20 acres that had been concealed lands.

It should be stressed the above is a hypothetical solution to the question of reconciling the pre- and post-Dissolution evidence for the Friary estate, but nonetheless the figures are a good match. See Table 3 for a summary of the Friary estate before the Dissolution, and Fig. 4 for the probable descent of the estate after 1538.

Is it possible to determine the locations of any of the Friary estate's land? The study of local toponymns does not provide much useful information for the immediate vicinity of the Friary, but it has highlighted Friars Thorne Farm as a possible location of Friary lands. No land in Table 3 can be placed in what is now considered to be Burnham Sutton, where the *Valor* stated part of the Friary estate lay. However, it could be that the Burnhams' parish boundaries were poorly defined in the sixteenth century (Burnham Sutton still had 'no particular boundaries' as late as *c*.1796), or they were highly interdigitated.[167]

The 1566 conveyance allows Vyncentes Close to be mapped to the south-west end of Friars Lane. This spot was still called 'Vincents Meadow' on the 1837 Burnham Westgate tithe map.[168] On the 1887 25 inch OS map (Norfolk VII.7; Burnham Westgate parcel no. 134) it had an area of 2.016 acres, a near-perfect match for its 2-acre stated extent in 1541. Vyncentes Close is just within Burnham Westgate according to Victorian parish boundaries, but in 1566 this area was probably considered as being in Burnham St Andrew's. Vyncentes Close remains pasture today, but is now part of a larger enclosure called 'Coke's Meadow.' Le Asshe Pightell cannot be located as yet. If it was in Burnham Westgate, then its 2 acres & 2 roods added to the 11 acres & 2 roods 'Land of the late Fryers within the feyld of Burnham Westgate' (item G, Table 3) gives 14 acres. This equals the *Valor*'s total for that parish.

Using the routes of various roads and tracks as reference points, and noting the orientation of the few open-field strips remaining on the enclosure award map, many of the parcels of friars' lands in the 1566 schedule can be roughly located (Fig. 5), including 54 out

---

[167] Williamson, 'The Landscape Contexts'. Under the 1821 Enclosure Act, powers were granted for the commissioner to shorten and straighten the parish boundaries (NRO C/Sca 2/61/1).

[168] NRO DN/TA 386.

Table 3. Lands associated with the Friary, hypothetically representing the friars' pre-Dissolution estate of 1535. One rood equals a quarter of an acre. To this must be added c.2 acres of their precinct including the site of their main buildings, which was not included in the Friary's entry in the *Valor*.

Lands/premises	Earliest date and reference	Area
(A) 3 acres with a house, located in Burnham (assumed to be within the precinct)	1541 grant to Cobham & Warner (absent from Jenyson conveyance, 1566)	3 acres
(B) 1 rood (with stable), opposite the gatehouse, therefore in Burnham Norton	1539–1541 Ministers' and Receivers' Accounts (absent from Jenyson conveyance, 1566)	1 rood
(C) 'Le Asshe Pightell', located in Burnham	1539–1541 Ministers' and Receivers' Accounts (absent from Jenyson conveyance, 1566)	2 acres & 2 roods
(D) 'Vyncentes Close', located in Burnham	1539–1541 Ministers' and Receivers' Accounts; 1541 grant to Cobham & Warner (also in Jenyson conveyance, 1566)	2 acres in most sources (one source states 3 acres)
(E) Lands assumed to be in Burnham Norton	1566 conveyance to Jenyson, parcels 1–54 & 56–61	45 acres & 1¼ roods
(F) Land in Deepdale Field, Burnham Deepdale	1566 conveyance to Jenyson, parcel 55	5 roods
(G) Lands in the field of Burnham Westgate	1566 conveyance to Jenyson, parcels 62–73	11 acres & 2 roods
(H) Concealed marshes in Burnham	1570 grant to Mynne & Hall	2 acres
Total area		67 acres & 3¼ roods (or possibly 68 acres & 3¼ roods if Vyncentes Close was 3 acres)

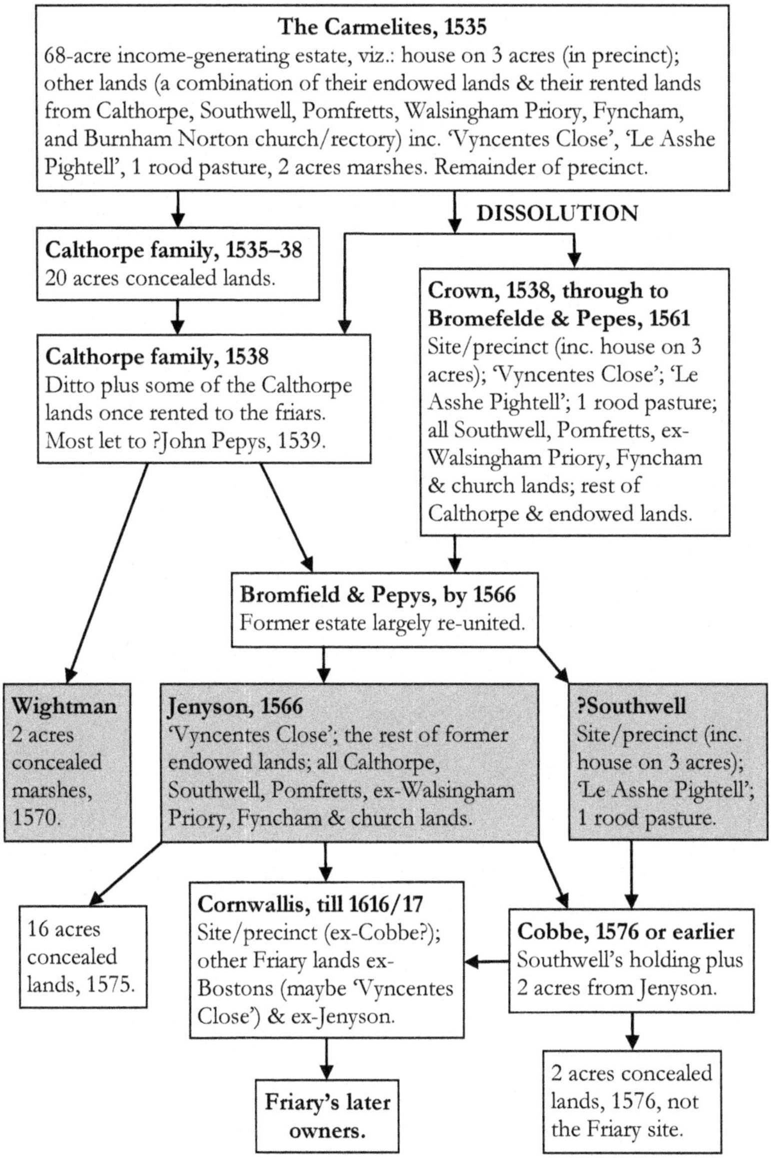

The Carmelites, 1535
68-acre income-generating estate, viz.: house on 3 acres (in precinct); other lands (a combination of their endowed lands & their rented lands from Calthorpe, Southwell, Pomfretts, Walsingham Priory, Fyncham, and Burnham Norton church/rectory) inc. 'Vyncentes Close', 'Le Asshe Pightell', 1 rood pasture, 2 acres marshes. Remainder of precinct.

DISSOLUTION

Calthorpe family, 1535–38
20 acres concealed lands.

Crown, 1538, through to Bromefelde & Pepes, 1561
Site/precinct (inc. house on 3 acres); 'Vyncentes Close'; 'Le Asshe Pightell'; 1 rood pasture; all Southwell, Pomfretts, ex-Walsingham Priory, Fyncham & church lands; rest of Calthorpe & endowed lands.

Calthorpe family, 1538
Ditto plus some of the Calthorpe lands once rented to the friars. Most let to ?John Pepys, 1539.

Bromfield & Pepys, by 1566
Former estate largely re-united.

Wightman
2 acres concealed marshes, 1570.

Jenyson, 1566
'Vyncentes Close'; the rest of former endowed lands; all Calthorpe, Southwell, Pomfretts, ex-Walsingham Priory, Fyncham & church lands.

?Southwell
Site/precinct (inc. house on 3 acres); 'Le Asshe Pightell'; 1 rood pasture.

16 acres concealed lands, 1575.

Cornwallis, till 1616/17
Site/precinct (ex-Cobbe?); other Friary lands ex-Bostons (maybe 'Vyncentes Close') & ex-Jenyson.

Cobbe, 1576 or earlier
Southwell's holding plus 2 acres from Jenyson.

Friary's later owners.

2 acres concealed lands, 1576, not the Friary site.

Figure 4. The Friary estate and the probable changes it underwent after the Dissolution. It is assumed that all the payments made in 1535 (except those to Carbrooke Preceptory and Hugh Thurlowe) were for rents of land. The shaded boxes are referred to, and their lands' areas enumerated, in Table 3. © The author.

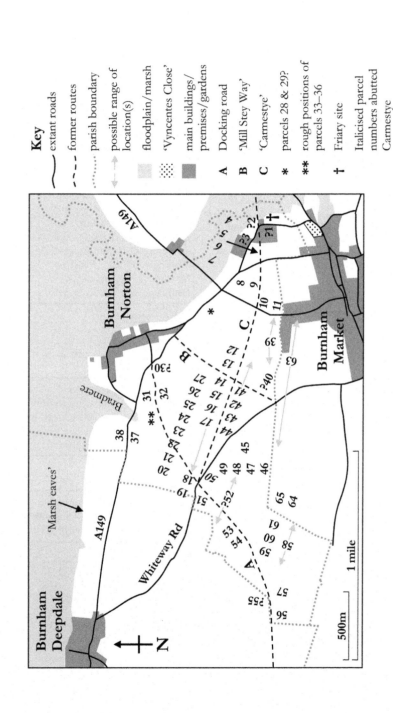

Key

	extant roads
	former routes
	parish boundary
↕	possible range of location(s)
	floodplain/marsh
	'Vyncentes Close'
	main buildings/ premises/gardens
A	Docking road
B	'Mill Stey Way'
C	'Carmestye'
✳	parcels 28 & 29?
✱✱	rough positions of parcels 33–36
†	Friary site
Italicised parcel numbers abutted Carmestye

Figure 5. Locations of the Friary estate. The parcels are numbered according to the schedule of lands from 1566. 'Vyncentes Close' is marked. The conjectured route of 'Mill Stey Way' is based on evidence from the *c.*1796 manorial survey map and Faden's 1797 map. Parcels that abutted each other: 2 & 3, 3 & 4–7, 6 & 7, 7 & 8, 12 & 13, 15 & 26 (end to end), 45 & 47, 45 & 48. Named parcels: 1 = 'Spryng Wells Yarde', 3 = 'Countes Acre', 21 = 'Scarte Acre'. Furlong information: 30 is at 'Roptell', 52 is in 'Breneshowe Furlong', 53 is in 'Oldhowe Furlong', 55 is in 'Deepdale Field', and 59–61 are in 'Puttockes Hill Furlong'. The latter was probably near to what is today called 'Hawkers Hill'. In the Eastern Counties and Midlands, historically, 'puttock' = a buzzard (Swainson, *Provincial Names of British Birds*, p.133); it might alternatively signify another bird of prey: a kite (Candler, 'East Anglian Field-Names', p.169). 'Sandepyrt Furlong' was probably immediately E of parcel 37. © The author.

of 60 in Burnham Norton. These parcels are scattered over what is the arable part of the parish, upland from the marshes, on sites ranging from 10–40m AOD. Mostly, they are on medium-heavy, chalky, silty loam soils, over a chalk subsoil.[169] This is the village's predominant soil-type, both reasonably tractable and reasonably fertile. Parcels 53 and 54 may have occupied clay loam to silty loam soil on unconsolidated fluvial deposits. This area, a field now called 'Brittle Lines' or 'Bric-o-Longs' ('Brick Kiln Land', *c.*1840),[170] is the heaviest land in the parish.[171] Parcels 50 & 52 may also have lain on similar soil. Such land, although fertile and moisture-retentive, has the disadvantage of being more difficult to work. Parcels 37 & 38 (and maybe some of 33–36) lie near a former sand pit, on light land, and 56 & 57 are on what is considered also to be some of the lightest land in Burnham Norton.[172] This kind of soil is easily tilled, but relatively infertile and drought-prone, and therefore is of lower quality than the rest.

Based on the names of two grazing marshes close to the Friary, it has recently been proposed that much of the Friary estate might have been waste land with no taxable value, unsuitable for arable agriculture.[173] The rent per acre of the land in the *Valor* cannot tell us anything about its quality, as it appears to be a typical figure based on customary or fixed rents and not (as would be the case today), a charge based on the lands' quality and whereabouts.[174] Although, currently, not all of the friars' former lands can be located, most have now been roughly mapped. They are not concentrated on the heaviest or lightest soils, in places far from the Friary or villages, nor

[169] Data from the UK Soil Observatory.

[170] Phoenetic spellings! Francis, *Clarky Bottoms and Small Hopes*, Plate 6.

[171] The author asked Winston Franklin and Alan Everitt, retired farm workers, who (and whose fathers) had worked on Norton Hall Farm, about the soil texture in various fields. The heavy land in Burnham Norton is not as heavy as that in some parts of Norfolk.

[172] Francis pers. ob.; Winston Franklin and Alan Everitt pers. comm. Likewise the light land in the parish is not as light as e.g. the soils of the Breckland.

[173] Chester-Kadwell, 'Site at Burnham Norton and its Landscape Context', pp.54–5.

[174] Mark Bailey pers. comm., 2 March 2021.

in flood-prone areas. Therefore, the new evidence gives no reason to suppose that the Friary estate was 'marginal land'.[175]

No known attempt at mapping the sixteenth century land holdings in the Burnhams has been published, although an unreferenced field book of 1596 was analysed with respect to Burnham Sutton.[176] Given a better understanding of the sixteenth-century geography of the Burnhams, especially of the furlong names and boundaries, it should be possible with the 1566 information to map precisely the friars' lands for the first time. This would confirm whether any of the (Burnham Westgate) arable land was in the region of Friars Thorne Farm.

The means by which the friars acquired their estate, or the dates when this happened, are poorly understood. In a recent analysis of some local wills, cash or goods (usually barley) was bequeathed to the Carmelites, not land.[177] There is documentary evidence for a gift of land (area unspecified), by Walter de Calthorpe, son of one of the founders, in 1247.[178] Three other donations of land occurred between 1298 and 1353, totalling 3 acres & 1 rood (3.25 acres) plus an unmeasured messuage and croft, but these are all believed to have added to the precinct or its environs. There is no evidence of any other gifts that would have led to the development of the Friary estate. It is probable, therefore, that the bulk of any lands donated to the friars was given, perhaps by the Friary's founders and maybe other low-status lords and freefolk, before the Statutes of Mortmain of 1279 and 1290 were enacted.[179] It could be that at least part of the Friary

---

[175] We can only assess the soil quality from its current state today, which may be different from the situation in the sixteenth century and earlier. For instance, the soil may have been amended by marling which ameliorated a low pH (soil acidity) and a light, sandy texture. Tom Williamson has also pointed out that the lightest soils may have eroded, so may not now be present in the quantities that they once were (pers. comm., 19 March 2021).

[176] Mentioned by Percival & Williamson, 'Early Fields and Medieval Furlongs', p.13.

[177] Alban, 'Benefactors Great and Small', pp.155–74.

[178] Lee-Warner, 'Calthorpes of Burnham', inter p.1 and p.2.

[179] Mark Bailey pers. comm., 2 March 2021. The Statutes of Mortmain were two pieces of legislation made by Edward I with the aim of preventing unregulated gifts of land being made to the clergy and religious orders.

estate was established as a source of financial support derived from rents when the brothers still lived as hermits at Bradmer.

We have seen that the Friary estate did not survive the Dissolution intact and it did not remain static afterwards. The 1566 schedule was the last to describe it in detail, and its subsequent history cannot be traced with the same level of accuracy. By 1675, with the sale to Tyndall (Phase *XIX*), the remains of the Friary estate might have been in two main units: first, the manor and site of the late Friary; and second, the messuage, tenement and farm of the late Friary, and its associated lands. It is unclear what the definitions of, and differences between, 'site' and 'messuage' are in the context of the documents. The manor's lands were not described in detail in the Tyndall sale nor in the trust deed of 1700 made by the Harrises. The manor's fate (if it was a separate part of the original Friary estate), after the Harrises' ownership, cannot be traced. The messuage, tenement and farm's story is more complete. It descended from 1689 through different owners to the Walpole family in 1725, remaining there for almost 200 years before becoming part of the Holkham estate. However, it was not being used as one farm. In 1689 there were two tenants occupying different portions of it, and by 1723, three portions existed, each with different occupiers. Its lands were in Burnhams St Andrew's, Norton, Sutton and Overy. It appears that the messuage, tenement and farm was an amalgamation of part of the old estate (and maybe also the site) of the Friary with additional, non-Carmelite lands, which had been bought, possibly by one of the Soames, or by Myddleton and Savile, before 1689.

The premises was known as 'Fryers Farme' in 1689, 'Friery Farme' in *c.*1720 and 'Friar's Farm' in 1843. Reference to the only Friary in the Burnhams would seem to suggest the ideal name for this farm, but some time before 1689 it was called 'Norton Farme' and in 1675 just 'Burnham Norton' or 'Nortons.' It is possible that the derivation of 'Nortons' comes not from the village name but from one of the former holders, Richard Norton, a man possibly from nearby South Creake.[180]

This was sometimes done not out of piety, but to free the donors from feudal duties to their overlord.

[180] The Pepys and Norton families, both from South Creake, had been, and would go on again to be, linked through marriage (Rye, *Visitacion of Norfolk*, pp.209, 220).

Alternatively, calling the premises just 'Burnham Norton' implies that the owner was an absentee with no knowledge of local place-names, and no ownership of other land holdings in the Burnhams. 'Burnham Norton' was description enough to distinguish it from the rest of their property, it seems.

The evidence presented here shows that various agricultural buildings including a barn and stables were associated with Friar's Farm. We know that a barn was constructed from the remains of the Friary church (see Sections 3.1 and 3.4). Historical maps show several structures on the Friary site and one map labels it 'Friars B^n' [Friars Barn] (see Section 3.3). The former location of these agricultural buildings is also confirmed by the statement of Victorian local archaeologist George Minns referring to 'the farmstead which lately occupied the site'.[181]

It might be assumed, seeing the site today, that all of the Carmelites' buildings were demolished or allowed to decay soon after the Dissolution and the site had no economic function. However, at least some of the buildings or their remains were adapted for secular uses which continued many years. Far from being the quiet and empty spot it is today, the Friary site in its farmyard phase would have been full of animals and people, with wagons, tumbrels, stacks, and all the smells and noises of a working farm. The 1720 legal case showed the pivotal role of sheep at the farm; the 1753 lease and 1843 sale particulars portray mixed farming, still centred on sheep.

Friar's Farm is now absent from the collective folk memory in the Burnhams. No details of the results of Savory's farm sale have been found, nor are there any records of Friar's Farm after 1843. Shortly after that, something happened (described in Chapter 3) that put paid to the site's agricultural phase and left the Friary as it appears today. The hustle and bustle of the busy farmyard was finished. The daily routines of feeding, milking, and mucking-out were over and the seasonal tasks of planting and threshing, lambing and shearing, no longer happened. The Friary site, apart from Friary Cottage, would now be bereft of people and activity for the first time in its long history.

---

[181] NRO WLP 17/6/40, 1047X3, letter dated 4 May 1868.

3

The fate of the Friary's buildings

3.1 INTRODUCTION

Physical and documentary evidence exists for several buildings at Burnham Norton Friary. The largest structure still standing today is the beautiful restored gatehouse of *c*.1320.[1] However, the extent of its restoration is not fully clear, nor do we know how much of it is pre-Dissolution in date. The gatehouse is architecturally important: 'If the restoration … is faithful to the original, its blank window replicas in proudwork on the west and east walls may represent the earliest use of that style as wall-surface decoration.'[2] The gatehouse first floor contained a chapel (mentioned in a Papal Indulgence of 1392),[3] within which was the Guild of St. Mary of Bedlam, or the Friars' Guild. This guild received bequests from local people between 1387 and 1517.[4]

---

1   Pevsner & Wilson, *Buildings of England, Norfolk 2*, pp.23, 231. For a full description of the buildings, see Heywood, 'Existing Remains Including Friary Cottage and Our Lady's Well'.

2   Hart, *Flint Flushwork*, p.44. Proudwork: a decorative construction technique similar to flushwork, except that the limestone patterns and tracery stand proud of the flint panels they surround. This technique when used to mimic blocked windows, as at the Friary gatehouse, forms detailing known as 'blind tracery'. Pierssené ('Burnham Norton Friary') suggested that only the 'front' of the gatehouse has been restored.

3   Bliss & Twemlow, *Calendar of Papal Registers*, vol. IV, p.433; Alban, 'Benefactors Great and Small', p.161. Indulgences were sometimes used to raise monies for building programmes (O'Sullivan, *In the Company of Preachers*, p.11).

4   Alban, 'Benefactors Great and Small', pp.162, 166.

An engraving of 1795 (Plate 5), showing the gatehouse before its restoration, has been studied and discussed in previous published works.[5] The engraving was reversed when printed, so shows a mirror image of the drawing it was based on, and of the true picture on the site.[6] In the engraving, the gatehouse upper storey is ruined, but its west gable survives nearly to ridge height though little detail of it can be deduced. Another building, now lost, stood immediately north of the gatehouse. The engraving's oblique view makes it impossible to see if this northern building was linked to the gatehouse or not. Close inspection of the engraving shows that the roadside wall associated with the northern building is of subtly different heights. There is also the hint of a possible small roadside door.

A second pictorial source of information for the Friary, which has been used in published research,[7] is a set of undated architect's drawings originally from the Walpole archives (Plate 6). These drawings closely match the current appearance of the gatehouse, and presumably were drawn to direct its restoration by Walpole's builders. In the absence of any contradictory evidence, the drawings naturally led to the assumption that they depict the original west window tracery still intact from the time the gatehouse was built.[8] As the tracery fell out in $c.$1940, and is now missing, it has been impossible for this assumption to be tested.

The Friary church, once possibly up to $c.$49m (160ft) long[9] with its nave measuring $c.$6.39 × 25.25m ($c.$21 × 83ft) internally,[10] was at

---

5   E.g. Heywood, 'Existing Remains Including Friary Cottage and Our Lady's Well', pp.86–91.

6   Heywood & Rogerson, 'Carmelite Friary Gatehouse, Burnham Norton'; Heywood, 'Existing Remains Including Friary Cottage and Our Lady's Well', p.99 n.2.

7   E.g. Heywood, 'Existing Remains Including Friary Cottage and Our Lady's Well', p.91.

8   E.g. Heywood, 'Existing Remains Including Friary Cottage and Our Lady's Well', p.89.

9   Chester-Kadwell, 'Friary Site at Burnham Norton and its Landscape Context', Fig. 3.13.

10   Francis, pers. ob., measured from the standing west wall to what is believed to be the remains of the walking space wall. Compare with the parish church's nave: $c.$5.46 × 18.09m (17ft 6ins × 59ft 4ins) internally. The choir/chancel lengths of the two churches cannot be compared because

Plate 5. The Friary gatehouse and barn in 1795. This is the reversed (true) version of the engraving: NMS NWHCM 1954.138.Todd14.Gallow.30. By permission of Norfolk Museums Service (Norwich Castle Museum & Art Gallery).

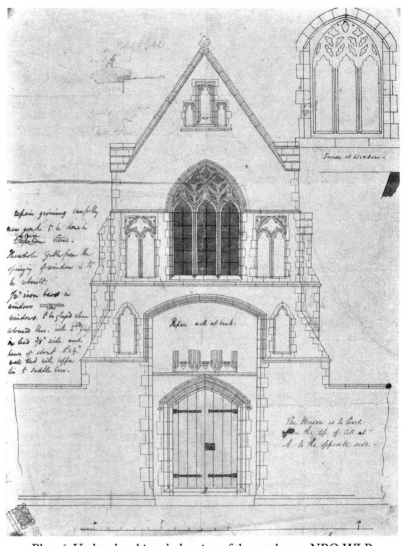

Plate 6. Undated architect's drawing of the gatehouse. NRO WLP 10/7, 1039X5. By permission of the Norfolk Record Office.

some point rebuilt as a barn. It has been claimed that it was 'converted in Tudor times into a house'.[11] However, the brick 'owl-gate' at the surviving gable's apex is an agricultural, rather than domestic, feature.[12] The church's remains, rebuilt as a barn with a ventilation slit and typical large barn door, appear on the 1795 engraving. Some commentators consider that the church fabric was still relatively complete before its re-use as a barn, and that the church therefore largely survived as the barn.[13] Nevertheless, the church must have fallen into disrepair before its conversion, because only the sill and bottom parts of the frame of its large west window remain in the barn's surviving west gable. The presence of a choir at the friars' church is noted in Sir Robert de Hemenhale's testament of 1391.[14]

Another standing survival is Friary Cottage, a heavily modified structure with a medieval core,[15] which may originally have been an infirmary, guesthouse or the prior's lodgings.[16] Pre-Dissolution limestone quoins (external corners) are present at Friary Cottage's north-east and south-east corners, but not at its west end. This shows that the building was once longer. Its west end decayed or was demolished, and the building was reconstructed in the late sixteenth century to the same width but a shorter length.[17] It was later increased in height.[18] A large buttress was erected against the north-east corner (using limestone ashlar from the Friary) at an unknown date. In 1970,

that of the parish church is truncated and its original extent is unknown. There are no visible features at the Friary to allow the measurement of its aisle (discussed on p.104).

[11] Moore, *St Margaret's Church Burnham Norton*, p.14.

[12] 'Owl-gate': dialect term for a small opening high in a traditional barn's gable wall which allows owls to enter and control any mice inside.

[13] Copsey, 'Burnham Norton: A Chronology', p.225.

[14] Alban, 'Benefactors Great and Small', p.160. Despite his wishes, Sir Robert may not have been buried at the Friary (*ibid.*, p.171).

[15] Heywood, 'Existing Remains Including Friary Cottage and Our Lady's Well', pp.94–6.

[16] NHLE 1013095; Francis, *Burnham Norton*, p.15; Emery 'Archaeological Surveys of the Burnham Norton Site', p.73.

[17] Emery, 'Archaeological Surveys of the Burnham Norton Site', p.72.

[18] Emery, 'Archaeological Surveys of the Burnham Norton Site', p.72; Heywood 'Existing Remains Including Friary Cottage and Our Lady's Well', p.94.

the house was extended and this led to the discovery of a blocked up spiral staircase in the south-east corner, within which a child's shoe (presumably an apotropaic object) was concealed. In 2011 the cottage's outbuilding was converted and linked to the house. The owners found several moulded pieces of limestone which they have displayed by building into the new work.

Comparison with plans of other Carmelite friaries suggests that Burnham Norton had at least a chapter house, dorter, refectory and a cloister (the last mentioned in 1492/3).[19] There is also evidence for a library,[20] and a guesthouse.[21] The buried remains of a large building of unknown function were discovered in the eastern part of the precinct in the 2017 magnetometry survey, together with other buried masonry remains south of the church (see Fig. 2).

To gain more knowledge on the Friary's buildings after the Dissolution, the following themes have been investigated here: (3.2) the date of, and reasons for, the gatehouse restoration, (3.3) evidence for buildings in historical maps and plans, (3.4) historical illustrations of the site, and (3.5) how the limestone from the Friary buildings was re-used in secular structures in the parish of Burnham Norton. The findings from all these investigations are then analysed below in Section 3.6.

3.2 THE DATE OF, AND REASONS FOR, THE GATEHOUSE RESTORATION

The Rev. Hugh Bryant claimed that the Friary gatehouse was repaired in 1840 when some excavations were made and skeletons unearthed, one of which was wearing a conventual habit[22] (though he gives no source for this information, and modern archaeologists are extremely sceptical). Unless the repairs were only minor, Bryant's date of 1840 seems unlikely, as the site was still a working farmyard until 1843 (see Section 2.3).

---

[19] Alban, 'Benefactors Great and Small', p.164.
[20] Copsey, 'Burnham Norton: A Chronology', pp.230, 237. Hulne Carmelite Friary's library contained 97 books (Holder, *Friaries of Medieval London*, p.98).
[21] Richard Copsey pers. comm., 7 May 2021.
[22] Bryant, *Churches of Norfolk*, p.22.

However, the Friary's future was under scrutiny in 1846. Henry Hill of Heacham was asked to visit the site and relate its potential for restoration. On 19 August that year, Hill reported to Walpole (the 3rd Earl of Orford), the site's owner:

> With regard to the Priory at Burnham Norton, I do not exactly know what your Lordship's wishes are: whether you think of placing what already exists into a sound state of repair; or to make an effectual restoration by repairing what is in existence, adding to it, and converting it to some practical use as school or almshouse ... The repair of the gateway merely as an Antiquarian relic would cost but little, the restoration such as I have alluded to would of course depend of the extent to which your Lordship was pleased to carry them ... It would be very easy to make a design for an almshouse in perfect keeping and in connection with the existing buildings ...[23]

Walpole evidently opted for the 'Antiquarian relic' option. The building work was undertaken by William Brown, a mason from King's Lynn, and possibly completed by late 1848.[24] In his letter to Walpole of 28 November that year, Brown does not mention the Friary by name, but he writes of two projects: one at Creake Abbey, and another place where 'there should be a door fitted to the North side to keep the Birds out of the upper room ...'[25] This sounds very like the first floor room of the Friary gatehouse. In a letter of 17 May 1849,[26] Brown thanked Walpole for payment for repairs to Creake Abbey and 'for fifty pounds in part payment of Restoring the Entrance to Burnham Priory ...', confirming that the two sites were worked on at much the same time. White's directory gives the restoration date as 1849.[27]

The local amateur archaeologist Rev. George Minns delivered a talk to a group of Norfolk & Norwich Archaeological Society members on their visit to the Friary in 1864, stating that during

[23] NRO WLP 8/86, 1045X2.
[24] Evidently a specialist in this kind of work, his firm went on to undertake important ecclesiastical contracts in Norfolk and beyond (e.g. *The Builder*, 16 (1858), pp.268, 280).
[25] NRO WLP 17/4/13, 1046X5.
[26] NRO WLP 17/4/13, 1046X5.
[27] White, *Directory of Norfolk* [1864], p.1009.

the 'gatehouse repairs', a new west window and niche above, plus flintwork and tracery on the east façade, were put in.[28] He further explained that the farm buildings were cleared from the Friary site at the same time.

3.3 ANALYSIS OF PLANS AND MAPS OF THE FRIARY SITE

Published and unpublished plans and maps are considered in this section, in chronological order, starting with the work of the Rev. Thomas Kerrich (1748–1828, a Norfolk-born antiquarian).[29] He produced three undated plans of the Friary (see Table 4 items F–H, pp.77–8), which have not been analysed in previous studies of the site. These cannot be later than 1828 in date, but could be as early as 1769 when it is known Kerrich visited the Friary remains and made sketches of them (Table 4 items E and O). The first plan (not illustrated) is a simple depiction of the precinct boundary, gatehouse and barn. The two buildings are represented by shaded rectangles, presumably to indicate they were roofed, or in the case of the gatehouse, to show that its vault covered an internal space. The second plan (not illustrated) is more detailed, and gives measurements for various features, but is drawn mostly in faint pencil and is difficult to read. It hints that some slight remains of the building discovered in the magnetometry survey, the proposed house on the 3 acres, may have been visible to Kerrich. The third plan (Table 4 item H; Plate 7) shows the gatehouse, barn, and several other structures at a larger, unspecified, scale. Walls are represented by either solid or dotted lines, but there is no key to their significance. However, solid lines are used to draw the gatehouse and the west wall of the barn, which are known pre-Dissolution structures. Dotted lines could indicate ruined walls, or standing features deemed

---

[28] The Rev. Minns' talk was reported in the *Norwich Mercury* (23 July 1864, p.6). In his 1863 excavation, he discovered a fragment of a female figure in alabaster, pieces of 'painted' glass, glazed floor tiles and a burial at the church's west end. The fate of Minns' finds is not known. Writing to the Hon. W.J. Walpole on 12 July 1866 (NRO WLP 17/6/40, 1047X3), Minns detailed his ideas for future work to excavate other parts of the church.

[29] *ODNB*, 'Kerrich, Thomas (1748–1828)'. He was born just a few miles from Burnham Norton, and was a prolific illustrator of antiquarian sites.

by Kerrich to be post-Dissolution. He shows the barn as an intact building in the first plan, so it seems likely that the combination of solid and dotted lines used to delineate it in the third plan mean it was built of a combination of pre- and post-Dissolution masonry. If this interpretation is correct, then the building to the north of the gatehouse (and abutting it on Kerrich's plan) is pre-Dissolution, as are north–south orientated structures to the east and to the north of the church. The latter may represent part of a covered walkway probably linking Friary Cottage to the east cloister walk and thence to the church.[30] All three of Kerrich's plans depict a now-missing wall extending southwards from the south-east corner of the church.

The earliest dated map showing the Friary more comprehensively is the enclosure map surveyed in 1825 (Plate 8).[31] It renders the site without the gatehouse, the roadside building to its north, or many of the other structures recorded by Kerrich. The barn (with an extension on its north side) is present, as are Friary Cottage and a small outbuilding to the cottage's north-east. The east end of the barn aligns roughly with the east end of Friary Cottage. The omission of the gatehouse in 1825 must have been accidental because it appears in other illustrations before that date, for example Kerrich's work of 1769 (Table 4). No part of the Friary site was affected by the enclosure, so its mapping may have been less accurate than that of the properties which were allotted or exchanged by the Enclosure Act.

The c.1840 tithe map (Plate 9) depicts additional structures, including the gatehouse, and shows the barn with an extended east end, but no northern extension. A narrow north–south orientated building occurs between the barn and Friary Cottage, but it is not quite in the same position as the one in Kerrich's plan (Plate 7). By c.1840, the roadside building north of the gatehouse no longer abutted it, and the long north–south building or feature to the east of the church drawn on Kerrich's plan was not there.

[30] Heywood, 'Existing Remains Including Friary Cottage and Our Lady's Well', pp.94, 99.

[31] The scale of two other early, dated, maps is too large to reveal the Friary's features in detail. These are: (i) Faden's 1797 map which labels the 'Friery' and shows three buildings there as black rectangles and a fourth as a little house symbol (Barringer, *Faden's Map of Norfolk*) and, (ii) Bryant's 1826 map which calls the site 'Friars Bⁿ [Barn]' and outlines a rectangular and an L-shaped building (Barringer, *Bryant's Map of Norfolk*).

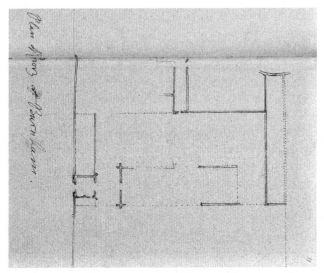

Plate 7. Plan of the Friary site by Rev. Thomas Kerrich, made no later than 1828 and possibly as early as 1769. Rotated so that north is uppermost. BL MS Add. 6759. fol. 11. © The British Library Board.

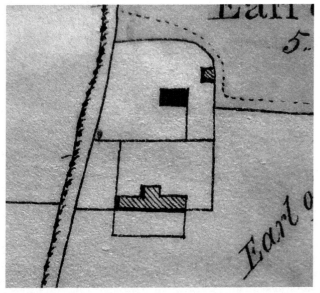

Plate 8. The Friary site from the parish enclosure award map (surveyed 1825). 'Burnham Inclosure Award 1826'. © The author.

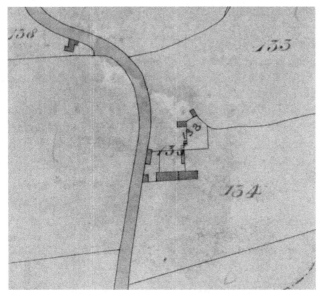

Plate 9. The Friary site from the parish tithe map (c.1840). NRO DN/
TA 229. By permission of the Norfolk Record Office.

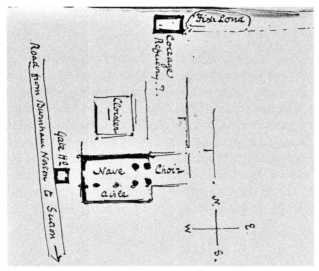

Plate 10. A sketch plan by Rev. George Minns (made either 1866 or 1868)
of his excavations of the Friary church. Rotated so that north is uppermost.
NRO WLP 17/6/40, 1047X3. By permission of the Norfolk Record Office.

A further, undated, sketch plan of the site has been located (Plate 10), annexed to letters from Minns written in 1866 and 1868.[32] In Autumn 1863 he excavated the site of the Friary church, uncovering the foundations of the nave's south aisle, bases of piers between the nave and aisle, plus the base of what he took to be a central tower.[33]

When the area was surveyed for the first edition 25 inch OS map in 1886, the only standing buildings at the Friary were the gatehouse, and Friary Cottage with its north-western outbuilding. The west gable was all that remained of the barn. Dotted lines on the OS map show the buried footings of demolished structures, many of which are on the site of the church.

3.4 ANALYSIS OF ILLUSTRATIONS OF THE FRIARY

This section concentrates on newly discovered images of the Friary pre-dating the gatehouse restoration (listed in Table 4). These are analysed below for the first time in the context of the site. Whilst it is true we cannot know whether artistic licence was applied by their creators, the pictorial sources still provide sufficient information about the gatehouse to enable comparisons to be made of its state before the 1848/9 restoration and its appearance today.

Kerrich's 1769 sketch and undated sketches

A sketch by Kerrich, dated 1769, illustrates the west side of the gatehouse and associated structures (Plate 11). It gives us a clear view of the gatehouse façade in the eighteenth century, providing information unapparent in the 1795 engraving. The 1769 sketch shows the west window's tracery had all but gone by then. Panels of blind tracery (proudwork) were present on each side of the west window, as today, but are only indicated by the very faintest of pencil marks and are hard to see without digital enhancement of the original sketch. Masonry is missing around the three niches above the door and part of the first floor vaulting has gone, exposing the niche bases to weathering. This

---

[32] NRO WLP 17/6/40, 1047X3 Letter, 12 July 1866, from George Minns to Hon. W.J. Walpole; and letter, 4 May 1868, from George Minns to Rev. E.B. Everard.

[33] *Norwich Mercury* 23 July 1864, p.6.

Table 4. Known illustrations and plans of the Friary before the 1848/9 gatehouse restoration.

Item	Creator	Date	Description	Location/reference
A	Bulwer, Rev. James (1794–1879)	No date. Probably after 1839	Gatehouse W façade, part of church/barn.	NMS NWHCM: 1954.138. Todd14. Gallow.27
B	Cotman, Miles Edward (1810–1858)	No date. By 1858	Gatehouse E façade.	NMS NWHCM: 1951.235.702. B6
C	Ditto	Ditto	Church/barn W gable end.	NMS NWHCM: 1951.235.702. B7
D	Hayles, Jane, after Kerrich, Rev. Thomas	1795	Reversed engraving. Gatehouse oblique view, northern building and church-barn. Described in previous studies of the Friary. Probably that listed by Woodward & Ewing (*Norfolk Topographer's Manual*, p.78).	NMS NWHCM: 1954.138. Todd14.Gallow.30 (and THEHM: DS.992).
E	Kerrich, Rev. Thomas (1748–1828)	1769	Gatehouse W façade, northern building.	BL MS Add. 6744. fol. 39
F	Ditto	No date. By 1828	First plan: precinct with E wall measurements.	BL MS Add. 6759. fol. 6
G	Ditto	Ditto	Second plan: precinct, rough sketch with measurements.	Ditto fol. 7
H	Ditto	Ditto	Third plan: Friary buildings.	Ditto fol. 11

(cont.)

Table 4 (cont.)

Item	Creator	Date	Description	Location/reference
I	Ditto	Ditto	Gatehouse W façade details I: blind tracery, window.	Ditto fol. 12
J	Ditto	Ditto	Gatehouse W façade details II: niches.	Ditto fol. 13
K	Ditto	Ditto	Gatehouse E façade details: blind tracery, upper & lower niches.	Ditto fol. 14
L	Ditto	Ditto	Gatehouse window tracery remnants?	Ditto fol. 15
M	Ditto	Ditto	Gatehouse vault diagram.	Ditto fol. 16
N	Ditto	Ditto	Church/barn mouldings and niche.	Ditto fol. 17
O	Ditto	1769	Gatehouse W façade details III.	Ditto fol. 18
P	Ditto	No date. By 1828	Three images: '[i] The ruins of Carmelite Convent at Burnham,[a] [ii] the ruins of the Carmelite's Church from the west, [iii] north east view of the remains of the Carmelite's Convent in Burnham from the low ground near the bank of the River.'	In unknown private ownership. In an album of material by Kerrich sold by Key's Auctioneers, Aylsham (Morningthorpe Manor Sale, 8th September 2016, lot 857).
Q	Unknown	No date. Assumed 1846–1848	Architect's drawings for the restoration of 'Burnham Priory' gateway. Described in previous studies of the Friary.	NRO WLP 10/7, 1039X5

[a] This might be the original on which the 1795 engraving was based.

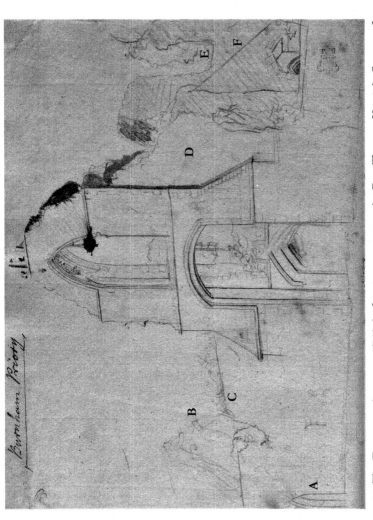

Plate 11. The Friary gatehouse in 1769, before its restoration, by Rev. Thomas Kerrich. See text for an explanation of the labelled items. BL MS Add. 6744. fol. 39. © The British Library Board.

could be why they are now so eroded, and why the words 'Repair wall at back' were written on the Walpole architect's drawings.

Kerrich shows the building to the north of the gatehouse (cf. the *c.*1840 tithe map, Plate 9), with a small arched doorway onto the road (Plate 11: A). This building might have been semi-derelict and open on its south side. The ends of what look like roof purlins (B) are depicted, though not in clear detail. A short length of masonry is missing, interrupting an otherwise intact eaves-height wall (C), which is slightly higher in the stretch adjacent to the gatehouse. These details are all a good match to the 1795 engraving's reversed (correct) version, and the small doorway's position is today evidenced by two pieces of limestone door-jamb in the extant wall.

On the south-west corner of the gatehouse, running alongside Friars Lane, are the remnants of a substantial and contiguous wall two storeys high (Plate 11: D), which is now gone. Kerrich's view suggests that there may have been a doorway on the first floor of the south wall of the gatehouse (E), positioned above the existing ground-floor south door. The first-floor doorway appears to have had a threshold and moulded dressings at its bottom right (east) corner. He also shows a diagonal mark (F) on the south façade, above the ground floor south door.

Kerrich's 1769 drawing of the architectural details on the gatehouse west façade (not illustrated; Table 4 item O) confirms that the panels of blind tracery were intact on each side of the west window opening. A clearer, undated, pen and ink drawing of these panels also shows that the upper central niche may have been flanked by further blind tracery (Plate 12). His view of details on the east façade (Plate 13) shows the original blind tracery intact, and one upper niche.

Bulwer's sketch

Bulwer's sketch of the west side of the gatehouse (Plate 14) is incorrectly entitled 'Burnham Norton Church (ruin)'. It was probably made after 1839, when he began assembling his 'Norfolk Collection' of pictures of local antiquarian sites and other places of interest.[34] Bulwer's work is exceptionally life-like, down to accurate detailing of individual pieces of freestone that can be identified in the building today. In general, his sketch shows increasing deterioration and loss of masonry in comparison with Kerrich's image of possibly 70 years

---

34 Campbell, 'James Bulwer fonds'.

Plate 12. Details of the west façade of the Friary gatehouse before its restoration, by Rev. Thomas Kerrich. BL MS Add. 6759. fol. 12. © The British Library Board.

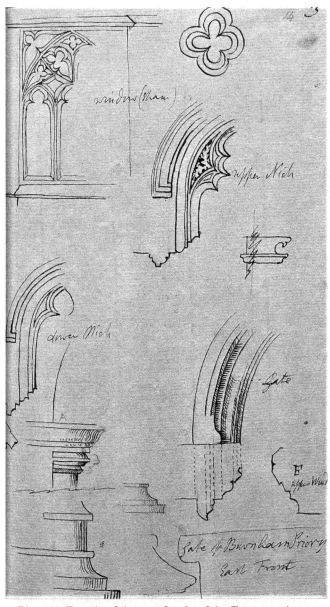

window (sham)

upper Nich

dower Nich

Gate

E
upper Wind

Gate of Burnham Priory
East Front

Plate 13. Details of the east façade of the Friary gatehouse before its restoration, by Rev. Thomas Kerrich. The blind tracery is shown in the top left corner of the sketch.
BL MS Add. 6759. fol. 14. © The British Library Board.

Plate 14. The west façade of the Friary gatehouse before its restoration, by Rev. James Bulwer. NMS NWHCM: 1954.138.Todd14.Gallow.27. By permission of Norfolk Museums Service (Norwich Castle Museum & Art Gallery).

Plate 15. The east façade of the Friary gatehouse before its restoration, attributed to Miles Cotman. The remains of a possible window opening are indicated by the arrow. NMS NWHCM: 1951.235.702. B6 By permission of Norfolk Museums Service (Norwich Castle Museum & Art Gallery).

earlier, but it broadly agrees with Kerrich, in that virtually no tracery survived in the west window. The perspective is slightly different, so some details shown by Kerrich cannot be seen in Bulwer's sketch, for example the south wall of the gatehouse and northern building. Bulwer shows the barn's gable end and part of its south wall.

Cotman's watercolours

An undated watercolour attributed to Miles Edward Cotman shows the east wall of the gatehouse (Plate 15). The watercolour accurately depicts pieces of freestone in the central door jambs and details of the angle buttresses, all of which are still present. The original upper part of the blind tracery had been lost, so the only intact tracery is the lower part above the central door. That door is shown as bricked-up, leaving only a small pedestrian opening. On the top left (north-east) corner of the upper storey wall are the slight remains of what might be part of the stone frame of a window. It is possible that it lit a staircase to the upper floor. Cotman's other watercolour (not illustrated; Table 4 item C) is of the west gable of the barn, the same as it is today, apart from the doorway being bricked-up (this was removed within living memory). In addition, there are a wall and features to the north, which may be sheds or muckheaps.

The implications of the findings that have been teased from all these illustrations are set out below (Section 3.6).

3.5 SURVEY OF RE-USED LIMESTONE IN STRUCTURES IN BURNHAM NORTON

The disappearance of many of the buildings on the Friary site points to deliberate demolition of structures for their materials, piecemeal stone robbing for smaller projects, and natural weathering and collapse, all alongside development of the site for agricultural use during its farmyard phase. Demolition materials from the Friary were re-used on the site (in the buttress at Friary Cottage for example), but they could also have been employed in the wider parish and in surrounding settlements. This was the case with stone from another north Norfolk village with monastic remains: Binham (Benedictine priory; 15.9km (9.9 miles) east of Burnham Norton), which was used to build a house in the nearby town of Wells.[35]

---

[35] NHLE 1014862.

The fabric of buildings from monastic, ecclesiastical and other high-status sites in Norfolk characteristically includes freestone from the Middle Jurassic Lincolnshire Limestone formation, absent from the natural local geology but imported into the area in the medieval period as a building stone.[36] Perhaps the most famous kind of this material was the hard and durable Barnack Ragstone from Barnack, Soke of Peterborough (now Northamptonshire). The limestone was fashioned into ashlar blocks, door- and window frames, mullions, tracery, arches, column components, architectural carvings, and other details, to be included in walling largely made of the ubiquitous Norfolk flint. Supplies of the best Barnack stone were exhausted by the latter half of the fifteenth century.[37]

It has to be admitted that the Friary might not have been the only local source of worked limestone. For example, there are at least four other medieval ecclesiastical buildings in the vicinity of Burnham Norton (see Fig. 1) which were ruinous by the end of the middle ages, and presumably easily exploited for their good stone. They include St Peter's church in Burnham Thorpe, which was consolidated with All Saints in that village in the reign of Edward I.[38] St Edmund's church in Burnham Westgate is somewhat controversial: it was either abandoned in the mid-fourteenth century,[39] or left to decay in the sixteenth century, but it still had a rector in 1685;[40] alternatively, it may never have had its own building.[41] St Andrew's church stood near the road from Burnham Ulph to Burnham Overy Town (now the B1155). It was annexed to St Clement's, Burnham Overy, in 1421, after which it was allowed to

---

36 Gallois, *Geology Around King's Lynn and the Wash*, p.175.
37 Alexander, 'Building Stone from the East Midlands Quarries', pp.115–16. Some Norfolk sites used Caen stone (an oolitic limestone) from northern France. The Walpole architect's drawing in Plate 6 reveals that Clipsham stone (from the same geological formation as Barnack stone, but quarried in Lincolnshire/Rutland) had been the original material specified for the gatehouse restoration. However, the word 'Clipsham' was crossed out and replaced by 'Caen' on the drawing.
38 Blomefield, *History of Norfolk*, vol. VII, p.14; NHER 1757.
39 NHER 1752.
40 Bryant, *Churches of Norfolk*, p.117.
41 St Edmund's was a portion of St Mary's Burnham Westgate, and the name of an area in Burnham for tithe-paying purposes (Rogerson, 'Burnhams from the Fifth to the Fourteenth Centuries', p.42 n.1).

fall into ruin, with its last rector recorded in 1447.[42] Peterstone priory, a house of Augustinian canons, was also nearby, in Burnham Overy parish.[43] The canons suffered badly from the Black Death in 1349 and flooding by the sea in the second half of the fourteenth century, circumstances that 'brought the house to its knees'. As a consequence it was annexed by Walsingham in 1449.[44] It is now a farm with only a few fragments of original masonry visible, the rest of the priory probably having been taken for secular use soon after its annexation. A further medieval ecclesiastical building survived for longer. St Ethelbert's (Albert's), parish church of Burnham Sutton, was largely demolished c.1771 to provide materials for repairing Burnham Ulph parish church,[45] but the stub of St Ethelbert's tower endured until the 1960s.

The Friary is closer to Burnham Norton village than are any of the above sites. It is therefore assumed that any limestone used in the village's buildings probably originally came from the Friary. Material robbed from the Friary is visible in various alterations in Friary Cottage, and in its garden walls, but the extent to which Friary stone was employed elsewhere in Burnham Norton has never been previously investigated. So, this is the first time that it has been possible to establish the types, dates and locations of the buildings and structures displaying re-used limestone, and to draw inferences from them.

Between autumn 2018 and 2020 the present author carried out a qualitative survey of accessible buildings and walls in Burnham Norton (other than at the Friary), searching for re-used pieces of limestone. In general the twentieth-century buildings in the village were not surveyed because they are not constructed of locally-sourced materials. Therefore, only those structures present on the second edition 25 inch OS maps (surveyed 1904, published 1906) were targeted. Some modern properties retain outbuildings that are on the second edition OS (and older) maps, so these were examined where possible. Garden and roadside walls made of vernacular materials bonded with lime mortar (indicating a probable latest date of the early twentieth century), and those with known histories of

[42] Blomefield, *History of Norfolk*, vol. VII, p.29; Bryant, *Churches of Norfolk*, p.4; NHER 1753.

[43] Bryant, *Churches of Norfolk*, pp.56, 58; NHER 1774.

[44] Midmer, *English Medieval Monasteries*, p.254.

[45] Bryant, *Churches of Norfolk*, p.61; NHER 1775.

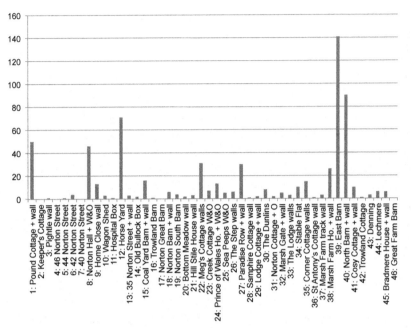

Figure 6. Total numbers of limestone pieces at each survey site.
This is the sum of the survey results for each site's main building,
together with results from any wall(s) and outbuildings(s)
there, designated W and O respectively. © The author.

construction, were surveyed. Only the outer faces of buildings' walls
could be seen, yet both faces of free-standing walls are visible. The
author was mindful that recording numbers of limestone fragments
on two faces of free-standing walls would bias the survey's results, so
only one face of each free-standing wall was studied. The research was
hindered in some instances by the presence of climbing plants, lichens
and render which obscured some masonry.[46] The results are listed in
Appendix 3 (together with OS references for each site's location),
presented in a bar chart in Fig. 6 and mapped in Fig. 7.

[46] It was not possible to measure the surveyed walls' areas, which would have
     allowed a calculation of numbers of limestone pieces per square metre of
     wall surface. This is why the survey is described as 'qualitative' above, rather
     than 'quantitative'. It should be noted that building materials removed from
     the Friary site would have included flint and maybe clunch in addition to

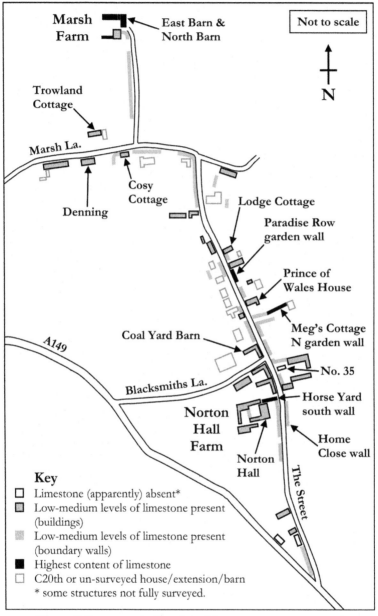

Figure 7. Structures in Burnham Norton containing re-used limestone. Modern houses are included as reference points, but, for clarity's sake, not their many outbuildings. © The author.

The survey found re-used limestone at 44 of the 46 sites surveyed, logging 669 pieces in total, with 20–30 additional stone voussoirs (wedge-shaped components of arches) reported by one property owner (but not all seen by the author). The limestone is unevenly distributed. Some of the older houses, for example Prince of Wales House (Site 24; Grade II listed, no. 1239089; seventeenth century in date), Lodge Cottage, Cosy Cottage, Trowland Cottage, Denning (road elevation) (Sites 29 & 41–43; all seventeenth/eighteenth century) and Norton Hall (Site 8; Grade II listed, no. 1238879; seventeenth century) contain very little limestone, sometimes just a single piece in an obvious repair or in blocked doors and windows but not in the main, older fabric of each house. With the exception of Norton Hall, these houses are mainly of coursed clunch (hard chalk used as a building material), which must have been obtained from a nearby chalk-pit rather than from the predominantly flint-built Friary. Of all the pre-1904 structures fully examined, only one cottage, No. 35 Norton Street (Site 13), contained no visible limestone at all. The cottage's original front and rear walls (later heightened) are of coursed, knapped flint with flint galleting,[47] and its original roadside gable carries a smart chequerboard design of knapped flint with burnt brick headers, again all galleted. Here, careful workmanship and emphasis on the decorative flint may mean that a mixture of recycled material from the old Friary did not meet the builders' needs, even if ex-Friary materials had been available at the time. Only one fully-surveyed barn (Great Farm Barn: Site 46) similarly lacked limestone. It is the furthest structure away from the village and the Friary, and its construction of clunch with several vitrified bricks must be due to its location beside a large chalk-pit and the site of the village's brickyard.

The house with the greatest number of limestone pieces is Pound Cottage in Friars Lane (Site 1), a former Walpole estate property,[48]

---

the characteristic limestone. This flint and clunch would have also been re-used, but is of course indistinguishable from flint and clunch from elsewhere. There is no evidence in the village of deliberate re-use solely of the limestone, apart from in the buttress at Friary Cottage. Maybe for that structure, it was felt that only the limestone was 'strong' enough for the job.

47 Galleting (alternatively, 'garreting'): flakes of flint, or pebbles, inserted flush into the wet mortar joints of (flint) walling during construction for decorative effect and to help prevent weathering.

48 NRO DN/TA 229.

Plate 16. A limestone carving re-used decoratively at
Pound Cottage, Friars Lane, Burnham Norton. © The author.

and the dwelling closest to the site apart from Friary Cottage. Pound
Cottage is the only structure surveyed in the village that contains a
piece of carved limestone historically re-used for purely decorative
effect (Plate 16); it might be the top of a column. Although outside
the survey area, an outbuilding at The Old Rectory, Overy Road,
Burnham Market (house listed Grade II, no. 1238875; TF 83741
42327; built after 1840),[49] close to the southern end of Friars Lane,
has the only other example of decorative re-use of medieval limestone
found so far: a section of limestone tracery repurposed as an air vent
(Plate 17). It must be noted that this building is near the site of
St Andrew's church, and so the tracery could originate from there.

The largest concentration of limestone away from the Friary site
occurs at Marsh Farm, especially in its outbuildings now converted
into residential use and known as East Barn and North Barn (Sites
39 & 40). These two buildings alone contain 33% of all the limestone
discovered in the survey. Here, the lower sections of some walls are
almost entirely of limestone, much of it rectangular in shape and laid

49 NRO DN/TA 358.

Plate 17. Limestone tracery re-used decoratively in an outbuilding at
The Old Rectory, Overy Road, Burnham Market. © The author.

in rough courses. Some blocks are very large, with one measuring
483 × 280mm (19 × 11ins). Also recorded was one rebated section of
mullion that might have come from a shuttered opening, or one with
glazing held in a wooden frame,[50] and two sections of hollow-chamfered
window mullion. There was additionally one octagonal block and two
further stones, one of which was a fine-textured grey material, that
might be parts of a circular column or columns. Using the dimensions
of the grey stone, which was visible in cross section, it might have
been part of a column whose original diameter (calculated using a
geometrical formula) was at least 19½ins. In the wall of East Barn, and
loose in the garden, were voussoirs from a large arch or window head.

When he converted East Barn into a home, its owner demolished
a short section of wall and discovered inside its core a piece of
limestone window tracery, with glazing grooves, mason's setting-out
marks on one face, and traces of whitewash still attached (Plate 18).
This is the only piece of curved tracery stone found in the survey
away from the Friary site. As noted by Mark Samuel in his study

[50] Stephen Heywood pers. comm., 4 February 2021.

of architectural elements from London's friaries, curved stones are difficult to re-use because of their shape, and were therefore broken up for rough foundation material, or re-used hidden inside the core of a wall,[51] as was the case for the East Barn stone. Also found in the same infill were moulded bricks from mullioned, glazed windows of two different designs, dating from c.1570.[52]

The second-largest assemblage of limestone including ashlar and rubble but also with some identifiable structural pieces, occurs in the south wall of the Horse Yard at Norton Hall Farm (Site 12). This limestone was used alongside flint, clunch and brick. Here, three sizes of plain-chamfered window mullion segments were present, together with several pieces of apparent plain-chamfered mullions without glazing grooves, which, it is conjectured, might possibly be from the Friary cloister.

Some limestone occurs in the buildings formerly of Norton Hall Farm, now converted into dwellings. In particular, the east range of Coal Yard Barn (Site 15; absent from the c.1840 tithe map, but bearing the graffito 'V R 1842')[53] contains several worked limestone blocks including another section of window mullion (plain-chamfered). The garden wall of Paradise Row (Site 27) also has limestone in comparative abundance. Other old roadside walls along Burnham Norton's main street are similarly and characteristically rich in limestone.

One mason's mark was found on a loose piece of tracery inside the Friary gatehouse, but whether this stone is medieval, or Victorian, is unknown. Rough 'X' marks were seen on two stones in walls in Friary Cottage's gardens. This mark, placed on a face that would have been invisible in the original medieval structures, indicated that the particular stone's shaping had been completed and it was ready to use.[54]

The identifiable architectural elements recorded in the survey are summarised in Table 5, and illustrated in Plates 18 & 19, and in Fig. 8. Finally, it is possible that the Collyweston-type stone tiles recorded from sites 24 and 25 in the survey may have come from the Friary.

---

51 Samuel, 'Architectural Fragments of the London Friaries', p.211.
52 Tony Minter (Bulmer Brick and Tile Company) pers. comm., 20 August 2021.
53 Francis, pers. ob.
54 Samuel, 'Architectural Fragments of the London Friaries', p.214.

Table 5. Identifiable architectural elements discovered in the stone survey at Burnham Norton, with two loose stones at Friary Cottage.

Item	Element	Size	Number and location
A	Rebated mullion, type I	6½ × 8⅜ins (cross-section)	1 at East Barn, Marsh Farm (Site 39)
B	Rebated mullion, type II	9 × 9½ins (cross-section)	1 at Friary Cottage, lying loose in the garden
C	Possible cloister mullions, plain-chamfered, no glazing grooves or rebates	8½ × 4ins (cross-section)	7 in the Horse Yard wall (Site 12) (some have rough, rather than worked, ends and may have resulted from the breaking up of longer original stones)
D	Window mullion, plain-chamfered, type I	7 × 4ins (cross-section)	2 in the Horse Yard wall (Site 12)
E	Window mullion, plain-chamfered, type II	9½ × 6ins (cross-section)	1 in the Horse Yard wall & 1 at Coal Yard Barn (Sites 12 & 15)
F	Window mullion, plain-chamfered, type III	9¾ × 6ins (cross-section)	1 in the Horse Yard wall (Site 12)
G	Window mullion, hollow-chamfered	7¾ × 4¼ins (cross-section)	2 at East Barn, Marsh Farm (Site 39)
H	Tracery section from an arched window, hollow-chamfered with cusping	See Plate 18	1 at East Barn, Marsh Farm (Site 39), found by the owner as infill when demolishing a short section of wall
I	Tracery section possibly from a square-headed window	See Plate 19	1 at Friary Cottage, recently dug up in the garden by the owners
J	Voussoirs, hollow-chamfered	14½ × 7¼ins (cross section)	20–30 at East Barn, Marsh Farm (Site 39), one built into barn wall, the others loose
K	Possible door jambs or window frames, plain-chamfered	Various sizes	3 in the Home Close wall & 1 at Coal Yard Barn (Sites 9 & 15)
L	Octagonal block, ?column element	8⅝ × 8⅝ins (cross-section)	1 at East Barn, Marsh Farm (Site 39)
M	Segmental block from a large circular column (fine textured, grey stone)	18½ × 6¾ins (cross-section)	1 at East Barn, Marsh Farm (Site 39)

Plate 18. A well-preserved piece of limestone window tracery, found re-used in wall infill at East Barn, Marsh Farm, Burnham Norton. See item H in Table 5. © The author.

Plate 19. Limestone tracery found in the garden at Friary Cottage. See item I in Table 5. © The author.

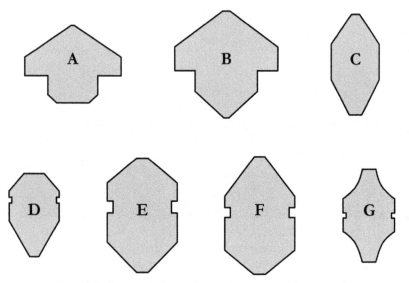

Figure 8. Cross-sections of some limestone architectural elements discovered in the Burnham Norton stone survey. See Table 5 for their dimensions and locations. © The author.

Plate 20. A cottage in Binham, Norfolk, showing re-used limestone quoins from the dissolved Priory. Such a pattern of re-use is absent in Burnham Norton. The piece of re-used limestone in the centre of the cottage's wall is carved with the date 1657. © The author.

A general pattern in Burnham Norton is that the majority of the salvaged limestone has been used in a manner described as 'casual',[55] with no attempt made to employ any of it for its original structural function (for example, in quoins, window or door openings), excepting part of a doorway inside East Barn. To understand whether this is typical locally, the survey results were compared with limestone re-usage at Binham, where a number of cottages show 'functional' stone re-use. Their quoins contain limestone ashlar originally from those of the monastic buildings (see Plate 20 for an example). This kind of re-use pattern has not been found in Burnham Norton.

3.6 DISCUSSION

A typical pattern of treatment of ex-religious sites after the Dissolution began with the roofing lead being removed, melted down on site and cast into ingots more convenient for transport. The bells, requiring specialist facilities for recycling, were taken away.[56] Although it was originally ordered that the monastic 'churches, steeples, cloisters, frater-houses, dormitories, chapter-houses, with all other houses' should all be razed, 'saving [only] them that be necessary for a farmer', in practice this could cost more than the resale value of the stone. Therefore, partial demolition was often undertaken by removing roofs and staircases to make the domestic buildings uninhabitable and the church unusable.[57] At Westacre Priory (Augustinian canons; 29.1km (18.1 miles) south of Burnham Norton), the dissolution commissioners spent five weeks suppressing, dissolving and defacing the site.[58] In addition to the actions of the commissioners and sites' grantees, there are also records of opportunistic damage and looting by local people at some dissolved religious houses.[59]

---

55 Parsons, *Stone: Quarrying and Building in England, A.D. 43–1525*, quoted in Heaton, 'Spolia Britannica'.
56 Lead melts at 327.5°C, bell metal at 1100°C. See also p.24 n.30, revealing how bells were transported from the area by sea.
57 Doggett, 'Demolition and Conversion of Former Monastic Buildings', pp.165–6.
58 Whyte, *Inhabiting the Landscape*, p.46.
59 The friaries of Norwich were looted (Clark, *Dissolution of the Monasteries*, p.390).

However, no single, common, sequence of events occurred at all the religious houses suppressed by Henry VIII. It would be wrong to assume they were all similarly demolished, or that they all had the same post-Dissolution histories. A few of the larger sites were converted into cathedrals with successors to the monks in the form of a body of secular clergy. This resulted in little destruction of their buildings, for example the former Benedictine priory at Norwich. At the university towns, new colleges were founded by adapting former monastic buildings, Christ Church, Oxford and Emmanuel College, Cambridge, being cases in point.[60] Other religious houses were modified into Royal residences, for example Reading Abbey, or converted by rich courtiers into magnificent country piles, like Beaulieu Abbey, Hampshire.[61] The City of Norwich bought the former Dominican friary for civic use, making it the 'most complete surviving medieval friary in England' today.[62] Other former monastic and mendicant houses had very different fates. Places near any of Henry VIII's building projects were often rapidly dismantled for their building materials, for example those in the vicinity of Oatlands or Nonsuch Palace.[63] The local availability of, and demand for, building stone would have impacted the survival of sites throughout the country. Elsewhere, a number of religious houses suffered from their local commissioner's over-zealous interpretation of his instructions to 'deface' them.[64]

Some special peculiarities seemed to have applied to friaries and not to monasteries. It will be recalled that the friaries' donations of alms stopped in 1537 (p.51), so the friars were impoverished compared with the monks who still had incomes from their more extensive and valuable land endowments. The friars' poverty drove some communities to disperse because they could not maintain the costs of running their household, and, in any case, they had already sold off most of their household goods.[65] This may have increased the probability

---

[60] Whitaker, *Raised from the Ruins*, pp.59–73.

[61] Whitaker, *Raised from the Ruins*, pp.87–93, 119–25.

[62] NHLE 1220456 (now called The Halls, Norwich).

[63] Whitaker, *Raised from the Ruins*, p.143; Clark, *Dissolution of the Monasteries*, p.392.

[64] E.g. the notorious Dr John London (Clark, *Dissolution of the Monasteries*, pp.387–90).

[65] Winchester Carmelite Friary had been empty for a long time before it was dissolved in spring 1538 (Clark, *Dissolution of the Monasteries*,

of their buildings being looted and damaged. The friars may have even begun selling off their house's fabric themselves, as was done by the Oxford Franciscans before they were suppressed,[66] again, adding to the potential for damage to buildings. However, in stark contrast to these scenarios, those buildings that the friars let on long leases survived the Dissolution and its immediate aftermath intact.[67]

It was ordered that Burnham Norton Friary should not be immediately defaced or demolished at its dissolution (see p.24). Its roofing lead seems to have been intact in 1541, implying that the buildings might still have been habitable. Their condition may have been poor though, bearing in mind the remaining four friars in 1538 could not afford to repair them. However, when the roofing lead was finally removed (it is not mentioned by 1544) the Friary buildings originally covered with it would have begun their inexorable journey towards dilapidation because of weathering, accelerated by people robbing the stone, and perhaps by deliberate demolition.

There is no evidence that the former claustral buildings at the Friary were converted into a sizeable residence before they had significantly deteriorated, as was done at some Norfolk sites, for example the refectory range at Horsham St Faith's Priory (Benedictine),[68] parts of the claustral ranges at Creake Abbey (Augustinian canons)[69] or the prior's lodgings and guests' accommodation at Castle Acre Priory (Cluniac),[70] all of which survive today with many medieval features intact. However, the practice of converting 'monastic complexes into fashionable country houses' was rare in Norfolk.[71]

Political and religious issues may have influenced the way the Friary's buildings fared. Spelman observed that in the beginning of Mary I's reign, Parliament was 'not willing to restore Popery ... unless they might be suffered to retain the lands which were lately taken

---

p.321). Inventory records that survive for some friaries show how the kitchens had been decommissioned before their dissolution because of the reduction in numbers of friars and sales of domestic goods and chattels to raise cash (*ibid.*, p.395).

[66] Clark, *Dissolution of the Monasteries*, p.353.

[67] Clark, *Dissolution of the Monasteries*, p.304.

[68] NHLE 1152454.

[69] NHLE 1015271 & NHLE 1342331.

[70] NHLE 1015870.

[71] Whyte, *Inhabiting the Landscape*, p.48.

from the monasteries.[72] The Pope had responded that the monastic houses, churches, and consecrated ground could not be given profane uses. The result was that the owners of such sites 'did not inhabit or build upon the houses, but forsook them for many years', unwilling to invest in assets with a doubtful future. Faced with such uncertainty, some owners demolished buildings that may have previously been in good condition, selling the building materials and giving themselves a cash windfall. Spelman describes how, for example, the owner of one former monastery in Derbyshire assembled a group of masons and carpenters and in one day pulled down that site's former church saying he 'would destroy the nest, for fear the birds [the monks] should build therein again.'[73]

Spelman also discusses the effects of superstitious beliefs, citing many cases of misfortune touching families that had acquired dissolved monasteries. These included children dying before their parents, sudden illnesses, incarceration in debtors' prisons, and fatal accidents.[74] At Binham Priory, its owner Edward Paston began clearing ground in readiness for building a mansion there, but a section of wall fell, and killed a workman. Paston 'perplexed by this accident at the beginning of this business' abandoned his plans immediately and permanently.[75] Spelman concluded,

> ... though the seats of these [dissolved] monasteries were in the fattest and choicest places ... it hath not happened that any of them, to my knowledge ... hath been the permanent habitation of any family of note, but, like desolate places, left to the farmers and husbandmen, no man adventuring to build or dwell upon them, for dread of infelicity that pursueth them.[76]

The farmers and husbandmen did indeed take over the Friary site, as shown in Section 2.3. What remained of the buildings was adapted for agricultural use, possibly with new structures being put up as and when the need arose. Perhaps these structures were built using earlier demolition rubble, and possibly on the Friary's footings.

---

72 Spelman, *History of Sacrilege*, p.239.
73 Spelman, *History of Sacrilege*, p.277.
74 Spelman, *History of Sacrilege*, pp.238–40.
75 Spelman, *History of Sacrilege*, pp.243–4.
76 Spelman, *History of Sacrilege*, p.238.

Changes to the Friary's buildings after the Dissolution have been investigated in this study using a combination of archival material, including maps and pictorial sources, as well as the survey of re-used limestone. The maps and pictorial sources are invaluable for understanding the gatehouse and wider site, though none have provided new information to aid our knowledge of Friary Cottage's development. The stone survey has allowed us to infer when the Friary buildings were demolished, and identify some of the details that they may have originally contained. The findings from this multidisciplinary approach will be assimilated and discussed by covering each building in turn beginning with the gatehouse, then finally turning to the implications of the findings of the stone survey.

* * *

The gatehouse once had an adjoining and contemporaneous room extending southwards as evidenced by its south door, which must have led into a room, long gone and not on any known map or plan, but postulated by Minns to be the Friary *portarium* (gatekeeper's lodge).[77] Kerrich's 1769 image suggests that the gatehouse's southern extension was more substantial than previously thought. It may have been of two storeys, its upper floor probably connected to the gatehouse chapel by an upper-storey door. A mass of masonry next to the field gate in the 1795 engraving suggests the extension's southern corner. Unfortunately, the area immediately south of the gatehouse was not fully covered by the magnetometry survey in 2017 because it was the compound for the builders' equipment during work on the precinct wall.

After the almost total destruction of the southern extension to the gatehouse, its roadside wall seems to have remained high enough to support an adjacent single-storey lean-to structure, the roofline of which is indicated by the diagonal mark (still just visible today) on Kerrich's 1769 sketch. In 1918, a 'respected parishioner' of the Burnhams related that in her great-grandfather's time, the gatehouse's lower storey remained intact, and was 'protected by a sloping thatched roof at no great distance from the ground'.[78] This may have been the lean-to structure.

---

77 *Norwich Mercury* 23 July 1864, p.6.
78 Sabin, 'Bare Ruin'd Choirs: Carmelite Friary at Burnham Norton', p.5.

Cotman's watercolour showing the altered east door suggests that by the early nineteenth century, the gatehouse was no longer being used as an entrance into the precinct. In any case, the west door of the gatehouse is too narrow to allow carts to pass through,[79] being only 1.47m (4ft 10ins) wide.[80] Perhaps its ground floor was used as a storage space during the site's farmyard phase. Then, the main entrance to the precinct would have been through a field gate some distance south of the gatehouse (see Plate 5), significantly further south than the present gate. In spring 2021, part of the garden wall at Friary Cottage north of the gatehouse was dismantled because of its poor condition, then rebuilt with its original stone. The present author noticed that one section of wall, $c.2.4$m ($c.7$ft 10ins) long, had brick foundations rather than flint like the rest. It was bounded by a block of limestone at its northern end. This might represent the remains of a carriage entrance into the precinct from Friars Lane.

By 1843 or shortly afterwards, the farmyard was disused and perhaps the buildings were run-down. The Friary's owner, Walpole, made a decision that would dramatically affect the site: it would no longer be a working farmstead. Although presented with the possibility of converting the farm buildings and gatehouse into a school or almshouse, he elected to restore the gatehouse as an 'Antiquarian relic' (above, p.71). Why was this choice made? Walpole's thinking has to be seen against the backdrop of the times in which he lived. The Oxford Movement within the Anglican church, antiquarianism, and the growing appreciation of church history and architecture all helped popularise 'Gothic Revival' architecture.[81] This was the chosen style for the new Palace of Westminster (from 1836), Victorian churches and civic buildings, and it catalysed the restoration of many medieval structures in Britain and on the continent. By the 1840s, the Gothic Revival had moved away from its focus on other Gothic styles and embraced the 'Second Pointed' ('Decorated') style, which

---

[79] Heywood, 'Existing Remains Including Friary Cottage and Our Lady's Well', p.86.

[80] Francis pers. ob.

[81] Gothic Revival was made fashionable by a member of the Walpole family, Horace Walpole (1717–1797) with his Strawberry Hill mansion (Middlesex; rebuilt from 1750). The style was popular throughout the nineteenth century.

had developed in the late-thirteenth century and flowered in the fourteenth.[82] By happy coincidence, this is the period during which the Friary gatehouse was originally built.

The 1848/9 'restoration' saved the gatehouse, making it the key feature of the Friary today, but it came at a cost. Evidence for structures closely associated with the gatehouse was largely obliterated, and the Friar's Farm buildings were cleared away. It also leaves us with the question: as a result of this antiquarian restoration, how much of what we see today in the gatehouse is pre-Dissolution fabric?

The newly-analysed pictorial evidence shows that the gatehouse had already lost its west window tracery before it was restored, meaning that the tracery that fell out c.1940 was a Victorian replacement and not a fourteenth-century survival. However, the sketches also show that blind tracery panels each side of the west window had survived complete until sometime probably after 1839, but whether they were still in place right up to the date of the restoration was unclear. However, close comparison of the Walpole plans with Kerrich's, Bulmer's and Cotman's work reveals new information not commented upon previously. A very faint pencil line on the Walpole plan of the west façade shows its dilapidated extremities before its restoration, and the line accords with the Bulwer sketch. The blind tracery panels either side of the window are inside this line, so must have still been intact at the time. The pencil line extends away from the south-west corner of the gatehouse and is labelled 'present line', showing that at least some of the masonry of the missing southern extension still stood. The words 'new quoined line' appear in the south corner on the plan, matching the gatehouse's current appearance. A similar faint pencil line on the plan of the east façade hints that only the bases of blind tracery there remained intact before the gatehouse was restored (and the words 'all new' have been written over the north-eastern angle buttress). This is evidence confirming that the west façade's blind tracery is indeed one of the earliest examples of its kind,[83] but suggests that the panels on the east façade are almost wholly Victorian. The extent of the 1848/9 restoration is summarised

[82] *Oxford Dictionary of Architecture* online version, search term: 'Gothic Revival'.

[83] As proposed by e.g. Hart, *Flint Flushwork*, p.44; Pevsner & Wilson, *Buildings of England, Norfolk 2*, p.231.

in Table 6, together with details of later work to the gatehouse. The new information on the gatehouse provides a clearer understanding the structure's evolution and will be useful to inform those undertaking future conservation work on the building.

We shall next consider the Friary church and its successor, the barn. As revealed in the 1541 grant of the Friary to Cobham and Warner (see Section 2.3, Phase *III*), the church once had a bell tower, and its bell or bells were sold in 1543. In 1863, the bases of four massive piers were discovered in the central part of the church by George Minns. It is therefore likely that the Friary church at Burnham Norton conformed to those of other friaries, having a choir at the eastern end, a central tower possibly with a walking place beneath, and a preaching nave. The earthworks of a southern extension to the church/barn are recorded on the 25 inch OS map, and may be the remains of an aisle. If this were so, it would have been an addition to the mid thirteenth-century church plan, which was comparable to the churches of two other early Carmelite houses: Hulne and Aylesford.[84] Aisles were not added to either of those two churches, but such extensions were a fairly common feature of fourteenth- and fifteenth-century Carmelite churches, for example in Sandwich Whitefriars (Kent).[85] It has recently been suggested that the Burnham Norton 'aisle-like addition' was more likely to have been from the post-Dissolution barn phase, but it could equally have been a late-medieval extension.[86] There have been no recent excavations of the church's site, but in 1863 Minns found the bases of three piers which could have formed the arcade between the nave and aisle, and reported that the barn's gable still contained the respond of an arch that once connected the church and aisle,[87] but this is no longer present.

Because of Burnham Norton's coastal location, it is possible that the Friary church tower could have been retained after the Dissolution as a sea-mark to aid shipping. There are other examples of this on the Norfolk coast, such as the tower at Blakeney Carmelite Friary which

[84] Clarke, 'Hermits to Whitefriars', pp.110–17.
[85] Clarke *et al.*, *Sandwich*, Fig. 6.18.
[86] Heywood, 'Existing Remains Including Friary Cottage and Our Lady's Well', p.99.
[87] *Norwich Mercury* 23 July 1864, p.6. Respond: a half-pier bonded into a wall to support the base of an arch.

Table 6. Summary of the 1848/9 gatehouse restoration, and other works.

Position	Date	Work
West (front, roadside) façade	1848/9	(i) The missing tracery in the upper storey west window opening was replaced; (ii) the damaged vault and the hole above the west doorway were repaired, but the former position of three statue niches was rebuilt as a blank flint panel; (iii) the ridge and eaves heights were established by building a new coped gable parapet; (iv) all remains of a substantial two-storey-height wall extending southwards along the line of the precinct wall were removed, and a new buttress created, dressed with new limestone; (v) a similar new limestone buttress was built on the north corner at first floor level, but with different detailing at its top.
South façade	Ditto	The largely missing upper storey wall was rebuilt to the new eaves height, removing any evidence of a possible first floor opening (though any remains of this opening may have already disappeared before 1848/9).
East (rear) façade	Ditto	(i) Brickwork was removed to re-open the original ground floor east door; (ii) the bases of existing blind tracery on the east wall were used to reconstruct the new tracery (but not to the same design as the original) and the central niche was re-created (again to a different pattern from the original); (iii) a new gable was built; (iv) missing masonry on the extremities of the two angle buttresses was replaced; (v) any possible traces of walls extending north and south from, and contiguous with, the east façade, were removed, making new quoins.
North façade	Ditto	The upper storey wall was rebuilt; in doing so, any traces of the staircase that would have given access to the gatehouse's upper room (the existence of which has been confirmed by Heywood and Rogerson's (1995) close observation of the masonry of this wall) were removed.
Roof	Ditto	A new timber roof, covered with peg tiles, was added.
West window	1950s	Wooden louvres were fitted to the window opening after the Victorian stone tracery fell out in c.1940.
Unknown	1970s	Essential repairs were carried out by Norfolk County Council with financial assistance from the Carmelite Order (Copsey, 'Burnham Norton: A Chronology', p.225).
West window	1995/6	New terracotta window tracery was installed, and the window was glazed. Designed by Ruth Blackman of Birdsall, Swash & Blackman Architects, instructed by Norfolk County Council (Stephen Heywood pers. comm., 12 November 2020).
Upper room	1995/6	New hand-made terracotta floor tiles were installed. This was part of the same project as the west window re-glazing.

was featured on a chart of 1693,[88] but later demolished. In King's Lynn, the Greyfriars' tower was preserved as a sea-mark, and survives to this day. Blakeney Friary church's position is uncertain, but it was probably at approximately TG 03214 44066.[89] This spot is halfway between the 10 and 20m AOD contours, only *c.*160m (175 yards) from the 'marsh eaves',[90] the boundary between the 'uplands' and the marshes, which are largely flat. On days of good visibility it might command an almost 180-degree horizontal field of view to the sea. Burnham Norton Friary's tower, by contrast, probably stood just below the 6m contour,[91] and was *c.*1.4km (0.87 miles) inland, as the crow flies, from a straight line drawn across the Burn estuary in line with the 'marsh eaves' to the east and west. Promontories on both sides of the estuary leave potentially just a *c.*36-degree horizontal field of view from the Friary to the sea. However, a local sailor has confirmed that there is no clear view up the Burn valley to the Friary, and that nowadays the most visible feature from the sea is Burnham Overy Staithe windmill (built 1816), standing at just over 10m AOD, directly north of the Friary.[92] These factors make the location of Burnham Norton Friary a poor choice for a sea-mark compared with the Blakeney site, so it seems doubtful that Burnham Norton's tower was retained for that purpose.

The remains of the Friary church were rebuilt as a barn, which was standing in 1795 (Plate 5). In the absence of archival evidence, the only signs that can help date the rebuilding are the bricks forming the gable parapet of the surviving part of the barn. The appearance and measurements of the bricks suggest a late sixteenth-century date.[93]

---

[88]   Cited in Wright, 'Blakeney Carmelite Friary', pp.14–15.

[89]   Based on a plan by Wright, 'Blakeney Carmelite Friary', p.29.

[90]   'Marsh eaves' is the local dialect term for the boundary between the uplands and marshland on the north Norfolk coast, i.e. the original strand-line of normal tides (see Fig. 5). Often this boundary is marked by a hedge or fence, and a significant change in elevation. It is a frontier between land that can be used for arable farming and habitation, and that which cannot. There does not appear to be a specific geographical term for this feature, so the dialect term is used here.

[91]   Chester-Kadwell, 'Friary Site at Burnham Norton and its Landscape Context', Fig. 3.12.

[92]   Henry Chamberlain pers. comm., 12 November 2020.

[93]   Peter Minter (Bulmer Brick and Tile Company) pers. comm., 26 April 2019. The brickwork detailing on the barn's west gable looks identical to

If they were newly made when used, this would give an approximate date for the conversion of the remains of the church into a barn. This, and the scant remains of the church's west window (see Section 3.1) mean that much of the church may have been largely pulled down before or around the end of the sixteenth century. It could be that there was a general campaign of demolition at the Friary after 1541, associated with the removal of its roofing lead. This was when the church, Friary Cottage's predecessor, and perhaps other buildings, were partially destroyed, with only structures of little value and/or most easily adapted for farm use being spared. The destruction could, however, have been caused, or continued, by Sir Charles Cornwallis, who was known to have 'wasted' the site before 1616/17 (see Section 2.3).

The barn was depicted on the c.1840 tithe map, but for how much longer did it survive intact? Recalling the sale particulars of 1843, Friary Farm's horse-powered threshing machine would have been, at this period, a substantial piece of fixed equipment, permanently installed in a barn, and it might even have occupied two floors.[94] It is likely that the only building on the site big enough to house it was the barn, which is evidence that it was still standing in 1843. The C-shaped flint wall recorded to the north of the barn by Brian Cushion (see Fig. 2),[95] and tentatively identified by Stephen Heywood as the Friary lavatorium 'with a structure around a well',[96] could instead be the remains of a roundhouse sheltering a horse gin to power the threshing machine.

Most of the barn was probably demolished during the clearance associated with the restoration of the gatehouse. It might be that Walpole only spared the barn's west gable wall because it contains recognisable parts of the Friary church: an original doorway, remains of the west window, buttresses and niches, which would have contributed aesthetically to his notion of the site as an 'Antiquarian

---

that on the former west gable of Friary Cottage (Plate 4), suggesting that the rebuilding of Friary Cottage took place at the same time that the barn was constructed.

94 MacDonald, 'Progress of the Early Threshing Machine', p.64.
95 Quoted in Emery, 'Archaeological Surveys of the Burnham Norton Site', p.70.
96 Heywood, 'Existing Remains Including Friary Cottage and Our Lady's Well', p.99.

relic.' It can be argued that perhaps nothing of the arcade between the church's nave and its south aisle survived above ground level, and there were no remains of the east window or other monastic features, otherwise Walpole would surely have retained them.

What can be said of the other buildings and structures on the Friary site? Though none of the maps and plans (or pictorial sources) studied here show the building that once stood in the 3-acre eastern portion of the precinct, possibly Lady Jane Calthorpe's residence, several other structures stood at the Friary site during its farmyard phase. The decision to clear the site in 1848/9 means we do not know to what degree the farm buildings were survivals of the Friary's pre-Dissolution fabric or if they were later structures with purely agricultural purposes. It appears they were viewed as being of little ornamental or historical value, adding nothing to Walpole's master plan. They may well have stood on older footings, but could have been constructed of a mishmash of earlier demolition rubble and new materials, or been so heavily altered or mutilated that they were no longer recognisable as being monastic in origin. Minns admitted 'the foundations of the farmstead which lately occupied the site makes it perplexing to determine the old work.'[97] Nevertheless, it is likely that the roadside building north of the gatehouse may have been medieval in date. This conclusion is based on Kerrich's plans, the building's Gothic doorway in his 1769 sketch, and cartographic evidence.

The precinct wall survives moderately well at the Friary, probably because it was maintained carefully to keep it stockproof. The precinct was indeed named 'Walled Yard' in 1825/6.[98] One $c.$50m length of the northern wall collapsed as recently as 1998; the remaining parts of the north and east walls were surveyed and consolidated by the Norfolk Archaeological Trust in 2016–2018. Today the east wall in particular, resplendent with its new lime mortar pointing, makes a striking visual impact against the greens and browns of the natural local landscape – on a sunny winter's day, a dazzling, white wall around the Whitefriars.

We have no archival information about how the stone, timber or other materials from demolished structures at the Friary was re-used after the Dissolution, but for sites where records do survive we learn,

97 NRO WLP 17/6/40, 1047X3, letter of 4 May 1868.
98 'Burnham Inclosure Award 1826' map.

for example, that the Leicester Greyfriars' stone was used to repair the parish church of St Martin and stone from Scarborough's friaries was used to mend its waterfront and pier.[99] In East Anglia, the original Barnack stone quarry having been long exhausted of its best stone, ex-monastic material was highly valued for prestigious construction projects and Cambridge colleges sourced it from the buildings of dissolved Fenland abbeys.[100]

The probable fate of building materials pillaged from Burnham Norton Friary has been traced in the survey of re-used limestone in the village. A large jumble of Friary limestone was used to build a massive buttress, and a smaller quantity of dressed stone to make an inglenook fireplace, at Friary Cottage. There is also much worked stone in the cottage's boundary walls and some loose in the gardens. Outside the Friary, robbed limestone has been re-used all over the village. Only two fully surveyed structures contained none at all, but it is striking how little limestone appears in the houses, with one exception: Pound Cottage (Site 1 in the stone survey). Unlike at Binham, there are no re-constructed limestone quoins away from the Friary site. Thus, the older houses in Burnham Norton may have been built well after the sixteenth-century demolitions of the Friary, but at a time when there were more surviving structures at Friar's Farm than there are at the site today. Pound Cottage's relatively high content of limestone, mixed with flint and other materials, may simply reflect its position as the house closest to the Friary site.

Most of the recorded limestone occurs in (former) agricultural structures and roadside walls. A large amount of well-preserved ashlar is in the walls of East and North Barns at Marsh Farm (Sites 39 & 40 in the stone survey), accounting for one third of all the limestone found in the survey. Compared with some of the damaged and weathered material found elsewhere, the ashlar there represents some of the finest quality stone salvaged from the Friary. This might indicate that it was taken away at a relatively early stage, when any

[99] O'Sullivan, 'Friars, Friaries and the Reformation', pp.304, 276.
[100] Alexander, 'Building Stone from the East Midlands Quarries', p.116. The re-use of timbers is poorly documented, but an interesting case was recently identified in Lincolnshire, using dendrochronology, of timbers from a priory being incorporated into a sixteenth-century house built in the same village (Gardiner, 'Twelfth-Century Timbers From Sixhills').

would-be builder could have carefully selected only the best stone, leaving the remainder for others to re-use at later dates either at Friar's Farm or elsewhere.

Marsh Farm has an interesting history. It was the site of Burnham Norton's staithe and is located next to what was once a large creek leading through the former saltmarshes to the sea. The farmhouse has a room dating to 1582 according to its owners, and was formerly a pub called the Golden Hind in commemoration of Drake's 1577–1580 circumnavigation.[101] Although a controversial land reclamation scheme of *c.*1641 prevented the village's fishermen from getting their boats close to their houses, there is evidence that it did not obstruct this particular staithe, suggesting that it had some importance then.[102] Eventually though, its connection to the sea was blocked when Norton Bank was constructed in 1822 and the saltmarshes reclaimed. East and North Barns were built between 1825 and *c.*1840 according to cartographic evidence, when two non-residential buildings to the south of the house were demolished and the farmhouse was reduced in size. It follows that the limestone in East and North Barns could have come from demolished buildings at Marsh Farm that contained ex-Friary limestone, rather than directly from the Friary itself. The remodelling process was probably connected with the premises' change of function from staithe to farm.

What might the demolished Marsh Farm buildings have been? There is an oral tradition in the village that a malthouse (maltings), a coal shed and fish-curing buildings once stood at Marsh Farm.[103] The premises was indeed listed as 'Malt House Farm' in the 1851 Census. Land immediately south of the farm was called 'Malthouse Meadow' and close by, Trowland Cottage (Site 42; see Fig. 7) was described as 'The Old Malthouse' in 1825/6.[104] More significant is a sale document of 1756, the details of which match it to Marsh Farm. Here, beside a large creek leading to the sea was a 'Dwellinghouse' and the 'Great

---

[101] The late Bridget Everitt pers. comm., 2007.

[102] The fishermen petitioned Parliament in 1641 about this scheme (Smith, 'Beyond the Sea Wall'). A survey of 1819 showed an 'old bank' with extensions running towards Marsh Farm, which would have still allowed the sea to reach it (NRO C/Sca 2/62).

[103] Francis, *Burnham Norton*, p.28.

[104] 'Burnham Inclosure Award 1826', pp.174–5. 'Old' here probably meaning 'former'.

Malthouse called Norton Malthouse ... together with the Kilns
Outhouses Edifices Buildings Yards and Gardens thereunto belonging'.[105] It is unlikely that the 'Great Malthouse' and 'The Old Malthouse'
were the same structure, based on the former's position near a large
creek suitable for ships and the latter's small size on the parish enclosure
and tithe maps. Nothing survives in the village today that could be
identified as a 'Great Malthouse' near a (former) creek: therefore the
two non-residential buildings shown south of the farmhouse in 1825
might represent its remains. At nearby Brancaster Staithe, the Roman
fort was robbed for stone in 1747 to build what was claimed to be the
country's biggest malthouse, situated at the staithe with the country's
largest trade in malt.[106] It is therefore conceivable that at Burnham
Norton, the Friary was similarly robbed before 1756 to build a 'Great
Malthouse' perhaps to replace the smaller 'Old Malthouse' and take
advantage of what appears to have been an extremely buoyant local
trade in the eighteenth century (and maybe previously), but one which
was no longer profitable in Burnham Norton in the nineteenth century.
Pound Cottage's construction date was probably similar. If Kerrich
had been born, and visited, the Friary only twenty years earlier than
he actually did, his sketches may have shown us a different picture of
the site: one with several more standing structures and remains.

Some walls in Burnham Norton contain recognisable limestone
architectural elements. Assuming these are from the Friary, they
show that it had several different designs of mullioned windows,
not all of them necessarily glazed; it also provides evidence for the
cloister, and suggests that there were circular columns somewhere on
the site (maybe in the church's aisle arcade). The paucity of re-used
decoratively carved or moulded stones in the stone survey results is
noteworthy. It could be that any decorative stones were unsentimen-
tally broken up and used for foundations or internal wall fill due to
their awkward shapes, so were invisible during the survey. This is true
of the piece of window tracery found re-used as wall infill at East

---

[105] NRO WAL 964/1. Rather than being a common staithe, open to all, it
seems to have been a private one. The sale document also includes the
'Creek leading from the Malthouse to the Sea', showing it was under
private ownership.

[106] NHER 1377. The Brancaster malthouse was 95m (104 yards) long and
9.3m (10.25 yards) wide. It survived until the nineteenth century.

Barn, Marsh Farm (Site 39). Alternatively, carved or moulded stones may well be 'hidden in plain sight' if their decorative faces were turned inwards when they were re-used, leaving a flat, smooth surface to any new walls.[107] However, very little decorative work might have been present in the original Friary buildings to begin with. It is thought that friary churches in East Anglia tended to have less extravagant decoration than contemporary local non-mendicant churches,[108] and it has been noted that friary churches were often simple buildings with little use of dressed or carved stone.[109]

The discovery of three Collyweston-type stone slates/tiles in Burnham Norton might suggest that such material was in use at the Friary, as was the case at the Dominican Friary at Thetford,[110] and perhaps also at Walsingham Greyfriars.[111] At Blakeney Friary, a combination of roofing materials was in use: lead, thatch and tile (but whether the tiles were ceramic/terracotta or stone is unspecified).[112]

The East Barn (Site 39) moulded bricks appear to be slightly too late in date to have come from the Friary's monastic phase. Their source is unknown, but since they occur with recycled limestone, presumably originally from a medieval building, a tantalising hypothesis is that they originated from the putative house that stood within the 3-acre portion of the precinct. If this is so, they might have been part of a post-Dissolution updating of its fenestration. It could be that salvaged building materials from this house (not definitively shown on Kerrich's plans and so probably demolished before 1769) were amongst those re-used at Marsh Farm.

[107] Victor Morgan pers. comm., 29 December 2021. Re-used abbey stone was surveyed in the Oxfordshire village of Eynsham, where, 'The display of moulded stones in walls and gateposts is very much a 20th/21st century fashion' (Parrinder, *Lost Abbey of Eynsham*, p.xvi), rather than a historic practice.

[108] Vinten, 'Friaries in East Anglia', p.43.

[109] O'Sullivan, *In the Company of Preachers*, p.19. Even the thirteenth-century friary buildings of London were 'plain' (Samuel, 'Architectural Fragments of the London Friaries', p.226).

[110] O'Sullivan, *In the Company of Preachers*, p.324.

[111] Giles Emery pers. comm., 8 February 2021.

[112] In 1543 (Wright, 'Blakeney Carmelite Friary', p.13). Norfolk's ubiquitous terracotta pantiles only began to be imported from the Low Countries in the seventeenth century. They were later made within the county.

Returning to the wider village, at some sites only rubble limestone was recorded. Limestone rubble was not used in local medieval high-status buildings, only ashlar, meaning the limestone must have been broken during demolition and/or was left exposed to winter weather and damaged by frost action. It is plausible that the stone was taken from demolished or decaying Friary buildings and used to build later agricultural buildings for Friar's Farm, which were then themselves demolished. In any case, the limestone, which had been so skilfully quarried, worked and shipped at great expense for the Carmelites, was now low-status rubble used merely as infill alongside other materials. This is illustrated in the Horse Yard southern wall at Norton Hall Farm (Site 12): the side facing the Hall's garden is of brick, whereas the limestone and mixed materials face the farm stables.

The final round of demolitions at the Friary in 1848/9 was associated with the restoration of the gatehouse. By then, many of today's stock of older village houses and agricultural buildings had already been constructed (based on evidence from the c.1840 tithe map). This is probably why the last of the rubble from Friar's Farm was built into the roadside walls along The Street in Burnham Norton.

A common factor connecting many of the limestone-rich walls in Burnham Norton is previous ownership by the Walpole estate, which owned the Friary between 1725 and 1922 (see Section 2.3, Phase *XXV*). Sites 8, 9 and 12 in the survey are all walls at or near Norton Hall, which was Walpole property.[113] Site 27 (Paradise Row's garden wall) in the survey was owned by Samuel Mayston or Maystone from c.1840 until 1852, when it was auctioned.[114] The buyer in 1852 is unknown, and no other public sales of the row are recorded until 2016 when Holkham Estate (the successor to the Walpole Estate) disposed of the cottages. Thus, Paradise Row may have been purchased by the Walpoles in 1852. The wall at Meg's Cottage, Site 22 in the survey (see Fig. 7), is at a premises formerly copyhold of Burnham Vewters manor, of which Walpole was lord.[115] Here were once two cottages.

[113] NRO DN/TA 229. By c.1840, Marsh Farm was part the Walpole estate, but was not in 1756.

[114] NRO DN/TA 229; *Norfolk News* 8 May 1852, p.1.

[115] 'Burnham Inclosure Award 1826', pp.201–2.

The western one, extant in 1816, was in ruins by 1886.[116] Some of its stone seems to have been re-used to build a pig sty on the site, and after that was demolished, the stone was re-used again in the garden wall.

Walpole's wall-building in the village gentrified the Hall, but his walls also had a more practical purpose. Cattle production expanded in Burnham Norton in the nineteenth century under Walpole as the principal landowner. After 1822, over 350 acres of fertile, newly reclaimed marsh land was added to the total available for seasonal cattle grazing and the local farmers became well known for their 'success at the Smithfield and other cattle exhibitions'.[117] The only route off the marshes was, and still is, along the village street, meaning large numbers of cattle were regularly driven along it. The present author last saw this happen about 25 years ago; these were boisterous occasions, showing the necessity of having strong roadside walls that the cattle cannot see over or through, and not just hedges or fences.

To complete this discussion of ex-Friary stone, we will now consider one last hypothesis: that some stone was re-used outside the village. We saw in Section 3.2 that the gatehouse was restored by the 3rd Earl of Orford. His successor (in 1858), Horatio William, the 4th Earl, was a lover of Gothic architecture and an 'acquisitive antiquarian', collecting architectural fragments from various sites across Norfolk. He eschewed the neo-classicism of Wolterton Hall, the Orfords' main seat, and instead made Mannington Hall (built c.1460) his residence. In 1864, using reset masonry elements from other buildings, he 'restored' Mannington (adding misogynistic inscriptions to the west façade).[118] Close by, Mannington's ruined parish church is 'surrounded by a curious romantic and picturesque display of antiquarian fragments, arches …' again collected by the 4th Earl.[119] To assemble this quantity of material must have taken time. Could it be that the impetus behind the gatehouse restoration was not the 3rd Earl (although he footed the bill), but instead his

---

[116] 'A Burnham Norton Estate. Declaration [and map] by Mr William B. Lane. 23 February 1886'.

[117] Kelly, *The Post Office Directory of Cambridge, Norfolk and Suffolk* [1864], p.196.

[118] NHER 6690.

[119] Pevsner & Wilson, *Buildings of England, Norfolk 1*, pp.605–6.

son, Horatio William, the future 4th Earl? It may be that during this work, some of the more 'choice' moulded stones or features from the Friary site were squirreled away by Horatio William to be used years later at Mannington.[120]

Thus, the buildings at Burnham Norton Friary underwent their own unique sequence of changes after 1538, influenced by a multiplicity of factors. These included the financial status of the last friars before the site was dissolved, the aims and ambitions of one of its founding families, the need for building stone for new structures in the village (itself dictated by alternations in economic and agricultural factors), and the Victorian popularity of antiquarianism. Although many of the Friary's buildings have now been lost from the site, their stone remains visible, re-used, all over the village.

---

[120] Long distance transport of stone by Norfolk antiquarians for re-use elsewhere was not unknown. Cart loads of 'sugar stone' were taken from the loose debris of the 'Porta Decumana' at Brancaster Roman fort by Rev. Henry Lee-Warner in 1848 and incorporated into a new barn at Thorpland, near Fakenham (approximately TF 93148 31773) (Lee-Warner, 'The Calthorps of Cockthorp', p.179 n.7). The distance between both sites is *c.*19.7km (12.2 miles) as the crow flies.

4

A new post-Dissolution
chronology of the Friary

This study of a Carmelite Friary at Burnham Norton in north
Norfolk has concentrated on the site's post-Dissolution history. It
is a period not commonly investigated for monastic or mendicant
sites, and especially not in the case of small sites like this friary. A
multi-disciplinary approach was taken by studying archival sources,
historical maps and images, oral history records, and surveying the
village for re-used ex-Friary building materials. Through the combination of these sources it can now be appreciated how the Friary's
many secular owners developed the site as a farmstead, how some
of the buildings changed over time whilst others were demolished,
and how the Friary's building materials were re-used throughout
the village. Moreover, hitherto unknown pre-Dissolution aspects of
the Friary have also been illuminated, for example features of the
Carmelites' estate, and tantalising details about their buildings.

Drawing together all the findings from this study, with recent
magnetometry data and other information, a new post-Dissolution
chronology of the Friary is presented below.

1538: Year of dissolution

We start with a conjectural description of the Friary as it probably
appeared in spring 1538. The largest building was the thirteenth-
century church, with its southern aisle and arcade of arches, central
bell tower (possibly octagonal, like those of other friary churches
in England) and lead roof.[1] Its nave alone was almost 20% wider

---

[1] Burnham Norton Friary church may have looked something like the one
that still stands at Atherstone, Warwickshire. Here, Augustinian friars

and 40% longer than that of the nearby parish church. The friars' church was probably divided by a walking space under the tower into the public nave and the friars' private choir. There was some painted glass in the windows, and at least one alabaster carving (inside the building, maybe from an altarpiece or a tomb), but the church was probably restrained in design and decoration. There might have been memorials inside to various Calthorpes and Hemenhales (members of the Friary's founding families), as well as to prominent Carmelites and other local worthies.

The fourteenth-century Friary gatehouse may have been one of the most ornate of the Carmelites' buildings. It connected to other structures of unknown, but probably medieval, date on its north and south sides, the latter being two storeys high. The cloister lay north of the church and its eastern range seems to have contained a two-storey building that linked the church to a separate building further north. The latter may have been the prior's lodgings, the guesthouse or infirmary.

Judging by discoveries of identifiable architectural elements in this study's survey of re-used stone, the Friary buildings, excepting the gatehouse, probably contained the minimum of expensive dressed limestone and had little architectural embellishment. Some of the Friary windows, as well as the cloister arcades, possibly exhibited plain chamfers as their only detailing.

North of the Friary's buildings, the land sloped steeply down towards a man-made water course and holy well, connecting to the River Burn. Beside this had been a once-important thoroughfare, busy with travellers and pilgrims, all of whom were a potentially rich source of alms for the Carmelites. However, by 1538, this route was perhaps no more than a track, and travellers crossed the Burn further south on the bridge and causeway built c.90 years previously by the prior of Walsingham.

The Friary precinct lay to the east and south of the main complex. It contained gardens, orchards, the cemetery, and a surprise: a large

---

took over and remodelled an independent chapel c.1375. The building, consisting of nave, central octagonal tower and chancel, survived the Dissolution and went on to be used as a parish church and grammar school. Some restoration work and rebuilding took place in the eighteenth and nineteenth centuries (NHLE 1365164).

building that might have been a house, possibly built to host the Friary's founders or other important visitors.

West from the precinct, on the other side of Friars Lane and opposite the gatehouse, stood the Friary's stable. The western part of the thoroughfare running past the Friary lay nearby. It was called 'Carmestye', and a fifth of the parcels of the Friary estate abutted it. Fifty-seven of these can now be mapped roughly and the pasture called 'Vyncentes Close' located accurately. Much of the estate was in the parish of Burnham Norton and was arable land. One parcel lay in Burnham Deepdale, and others may have been near Friars Thorne Farm in Burnham Westgate.

The standard of living of the last four friars in 1538 can only be guessed at, since no archival evidence survives to inform us. With no known bequests after 1532, the friars must have relied on alms, their estate's rental income and they may have also leased out parts of their precinct. Despite this, they could not survive the catastrophic financial challenge that all friaries were to encounter: the cessation of alms-giving by laypeople from winter 1537 onwards. The friars could not meet the costs of running and maintaining their buildings and were willing to transfer them to Lady Jane Calthorpe, the widow of a descendant of one of the founders. The Friary was abandoned and silent by the end of 1538, and the last four friars disappeared into obscurity. They may have received some small gift out of the house's petty cash when they left, but, unlike many of the monks, no pension was provided for them.[2] The Friary buildings were neither razed nor defaced.

After 1538 to end of sixteenth century

As early at 1539, Lady Jane was a tenant or occupier of the former Friary. The friars' old estate was already broken up, partly by the Carmelites secretly granting or leasing 20 acres of it shortly before the house was dissolved, and partly by some rented lands returning to the Calthorpe family. We do not know for how long the buildings remained untouched, but it is likely the lead roofs were stripped away in 1541. By this stage, Lady Jane was also the tenant of a house on 3 acres of land associated with the Friary estate. The archival sources do not detail the location of this house, but it could correspond with the

---

[2]   Clark, *Dissolution of the Monasteries*, pp.444–6.

large building that once stood in the east part of the precinct. Lady Jane still retained the house in 1544. It endured until 1561, but its later history is unknown and it did not feature in eighteenth-century depictions of the site. The masonry remains found in the eastern part of the precinct are a prime target for thorough excavation at some future date.

If the church had not already been demolished to prevent any future re-establishment of the Friary, or begun collapsing after several decades without a roof, it might have been destroyed by Sir Charles Cornwallis who 'wasted' the site before 1616/17. However, any buildings that could be easily adapted for secular purposes probably were left standing.

The ruined Friary church was finally rebuilt into a barn, and, probably at the same time, the remains of another structure (possibly the prior's lodgings, the Friary's guesthouse or infirmary) were rebuilt as a cottage (Friary Cottage) by the end of the century. The new barn probably matched the church's original footprint, but Friary Cottage represents a truncated version of its predecessor building. The site was now a farmstead. As far as we are aware, no claustral buildings were converted from a relatively intact state into any kind of notable residence. Conceivably there was no need for this to happen, with there already being a potentially good house on the 3-acre plot just to the east of the main Friary buildings.

Seventeenth and eighteenth centuries

The Friary site went through a complex sequence of ownership amongst interrelated families before finally being absorbed into the Walpoles' expanding estate. The farmstead was known simply as 'Nortons' in 1675 and only acquired the more suitable name 'Fryers Farme' from around 1689. It now comprised arable land, sheep feedings, fresh marshes, saltmarshes, and a meadow that lay in Burnhams Norton, St Andrews, Sutton and Overy. By 1753, the farm was enlarged by amalgamation with two additional tenements.

What little we know of the Friary buildings during this stage is entirely thanks to the sketches made by the antiquarian Thomas Kerrich, starting in 1769. At that stage, the gatehouse's southern extension was largely gone and the gatehouse itself was roofless. Its upper storey was falling down, though its proudwork was still intact. The northern extension of the gatehouse appears to have been semi-derelict; only half of it was still roofed. North of the barn a structure which might have derived from the cloister's east range was still standing, as were unidentified features east of the barn.

Worked limestone probably originating from the site's medieval buildings was re-used in secular structures all over the village. A large amount of high-quality ashlar was taken to Marsh Farm, which was then a staithe. There, the stone was probably used to build a 'Great Malthouse', extant in 1756. Pound Cottage was probably built at around the same time, and it contains a sizeable quantity of limestone. Interestingly, the other old houses in Burnham Norton contain insignificant amounts of Friary limestone, all of it used 'casually' as general wall infill especially in repairs or modifications, save for the carving displayed at Pound Cottage. By contrast, at nearby Binham, salvaged limestone from its Priory exhibits a different, 'functional', pattern of use as exemplified by several cottages with limestone quoins.

Nineteenth century

Significant changes happened in the village, which impacted on the uses of ex-Friary limestone. Saltmarshes were reclaimed in 1822, and the parish was enclosed four years later. The old staithe was now landlocked, becoming Marsh Farm. The 'Great Malthouse,' or its remains, was demolished and its materials recycled into a new barn and cattle sheds, which all display a large amount of worked limestone. Carmestye was closed as a public road and its route ploughed up.

The gatehouse continued deteriorating. The six other standing buildings at the Friary in *c.*1840 were: Friary Cottage; the barn; the gatehouse's northern extension; part of what was, possibly, the east claustral range; a probable privy; and a small building north-east of Friary Cottage.

'Friar's Farm' lasted until 1843, when its final tenant relinquished his lease and held a dispersal sale. It had been a mixed farm typical of the district, producing barley and turnips and supporting 325 head of sheep but just 17 cattle. Its buildings would have included implement sheds and stabling, perhaps set amongst some ivy-covered stubs of ruined medieval walls. The barn probably housed a large threshing machine, and close to its north wall lie footings that might relate to the machine's four-horse gin.

The farm was erased from the village when its owners, the Walpole family, transformed its site into an 'Antiquarian relic'. The gatehouse was restored in 1848/9 but most other structures at the Friary, except the church/barn's west wall and Friary Cottage, were demolished and cleared away. There is a possibility that some Gothic architectural features may have been removed from the site and used as adornments in a later restoration of another Walpole property: Mannington Hall. It is now hard to imagine the Friary site as a working farm. What medieval fabric the farm buildings contained, if any, is unknown, but they would have helped us to understand the site's layout and evolution. However, nineteenth-century antiquarianism has destroyed the evidence.

With most of Burnham Norton's older housing already built, the site clearance rubble was probably used in new agricultural buildings and walls associated with Norton Hall Farm's cattle production. Unlike that at Marsh Farm, much of the limestone in these walls is poor in quality. Maybe it had lain in rubble heaps at Friar's Farm, exposed to frost for many years. Alternatively, the stones may have been damaged by two rounds of demolition: first of the Carmelites' original buildings, and second, of the farm buildings into which they were recycled.

Time has mellowed the gatehouse restoration work, and it was unappreciated how much of the current fabric is medieval and how much Victorian. We can now say that Walpole rebuilt much of the first floor, installed new window tracery, re-roofed the structure, and tidied up the corners of the gatehouse by building new quoins. Without the restoration work, the gatehouse's medieval proudwork and vault might well have been lost by now.

The holy well (the spring) at the Friary was recorded for the first time as a place of resort for local people.

Twentieth century to present

In 1917 the chime of a bell resounded from the precinct for the first time since the Dissolution. However, it was not to mark the Holy Offices as had happened during the Carmelites' residence but had the wholly secular purpose of regulating the daily routine in the German prisoners-of-war camp at the Friary site. The exact location, and the duration, of the camp's fenced compound of tents remains unknown but it was probably towards the west, the driest part of the precinct though away from the site of the Friary buildings. Bespoke pottery and tokens were made to be used in the camp.

The isolated setting of the Friary was completely altered in the 1950s when the new Burnham Market school was built opposite the gatehouse, and this obliterated any remains of the Friary stable. By this time, the Victorian tracery had fallen from the gatehouse window and wooden louvres were put in place.

The holy well continued to hold significance for residents of the Burnhams.

Some aspect of the Friary's former Christian spirituality was briefly recovered when, in 1977, Friary Cottage's owner, herself a Carmelite Tertiary, instigated services in the gatehouse.

In 1995/6, under the care of Norfolk County Council, a steel spiral staircase was constructed for the gatehouse first floor room. Bespoke terracotta floor tiles and window tracery was installed, and the gatehouse west window glazed. This made the room accessible and gives a feel of what the space was like when it was a guild chapel. In 2010, the Friary and precinct were leased to the Norfolk Archaeological Trust, under whose guardianship the precinct walls were surveyed and consolidated and the site covered by a magnetometry survey.

Concluding remarks

Many of the country's monastic remains are presented to the public as beautiful ruins set against a peaceful backdrop of neatly mown grass, carefully fenced off from the modern world. Their post-Dissolution features and modifications have in many cases been stripped away to emphasise the medieval fabric, or in an attempt to create a picturesque ideal. It is fair to say that this approach has led to many sites' post-Dissolution histories being largely ignored. It creates the misleading impression that sites were totally abandoned once their religious communities left, and that no uses were found for them apart from perhaps as a stone quarry or as a subject for artists. This is not necessarily the case, as revealed in this book.

Studying the neglected post-Dissolution phase of Burnham Norton Friary's story has revealed a rich sequence of changes and alterations caused by the many owners' different plans and priorities for the site. It has shed much detail on the Friary's earlier history too. It is hoped that this book may prove a timely catalyst for others to carry out similarly fruitful studies elsewhere.

Appendix 1 The Friary's holy well and springs

The springs and holy well associated with the Friary are intrinsic to an understanding of the site as a whole. Several springs (known to some local people as 'Friars Springs') rise in hollows to the north of Friary Cottage, and their water flows along a pebbly channel ('The Canal') that connects to the River Burn.[1] One spring comes up in, and fills, a small rectangular limestone cistern in the bed of The Canal and is identified as a holy well (Plate 21). Inside, pinhead-sized specks of flint gyrate in the eddies of the upwelling spring, and are captivating to watch. The ebullient water used to overtop the mossy edges of the cistern,[2] though now it exits through a break in its side.[3] The holy well is shaded by trees and is close to lush beds of watercress.

The early history of the springs, and whether any of them had sacred connotations before the Friary was built, is unknown. Assuming they flowed historically as they still do today, they would have formed an invaluable watering place for people and their animals crossing the River Burn valley via the now-lost thoroughfare and ford (see Fig. 1 and p.3), as well as for the villagers and livestock at Burnham Norton. At this early date, during the first half of the thirteenth century, the Burn valley was still tidal and the springs probably emptied into a small, winding creek, a tributary of the river. If this creek was large enough to be navigable at high water,

---

[1] At least one other spring rises just east of Friary Cottage. All these springs including the holy well are on private land. The Canal was, according to local tradition, straightened and widened when the Friary was built to allow stone-carrying barges to reach the construction site (NHLE 1013095; Pierssené, 'Burnham Norton Friary'). Note that The Canal is sometimes confused with the canalised section of the Burn, to the immediate north of the Union Mills in Burnham Overy Town, but the two are different places.

[2] NHLE 1013095.

[3] Francis pers. ob.

Plate 21. The Friary holy well, looking towards the east. © The author.

there may have been a small staithe near the springs or perhaps just a simple 'hard' where the villagers could land their boats. Back then, it would have been part of an open, treeless, landscape of grazed saltmarsh vegetation.

An argument has been put forward that the spring(s) could not have been used when the Burn estuary was tidal because of salt water contamination. However, local knowledge proves that this is incorrect. Springs in the saltmarsh at Brancaster Staithe were once the source of drinking water for people living in the cottages there and were easily accessed at low water. Such springs can quickly flush away the sea water once the tide begins to ebb.[4] In addition, if an adequate timber or masonry well-head was provided, sea water could be completely excluded from a spring at any state of the tide.

No foundation charter survives for the Friary, but quite possibly the springs were granted specifically to the Carmelites for their water supply when they moved to the Burn valley site in 1253. Historic England's listing document for the Friary states that for springs it is 'quite rare in Eastern England for religious orders to adopt them

---

4   Francis family recollections, unpublished. One of the springs at Brancaster Staithe was important and permanent enough to be named: 'The Judy' (Amanda Loose pers. comm., 2020).

and incorporate them within their precincts',[5] and that the principal spring being 'taken up in this way in the 13th century, and then by an order of friars, is most unusual.'[6] However, it is thought that many springs were designated as holy wells between 1200 and 1500,[7] so maybe the Carmelites themselves pronounced the spring as sacred. The spring might have been a pilgrimage site and Friary Cottage's predecessor may have been built as not just an ordinary guesthouse, but one specifically for visitors to the holy well.[8] It is interesting to speculate on the status of the spring after the new bridge was built across the Burn by the prior of Walsingham in the fifteenth century (p.8). Arguably, this act removed most of the Friary's passing traffic, and presumably reduced alms donations as a result. If the spring was not already regarded as a holy well, it might have been promoted as one by the friars then as a direct response to the effects of the new bridge and an attempt to compensate for their loss of income. Any structures at the holy well associated with its identity as a pilgrimage site or shrine would have been later swept away by reformist commissioners.

The earliest documentary record of the springs at Burnham Norton Friary is the toponym 'Spryng Wells Yarde' that occurs in the 1566 schedule of lands that once belonged to the Carmelites (see p.31). Although it is tempting to assume that this small (1 rood, or 0.25 acres) parcel of land must be the space between Friary Cottage and the holy well, Spryng Wells Yarde was located on the west side of Friars Lane according to the schedule's description. Here, the author knows of no natural springs and the elevation is higher than on the east of the lane. It seems likely that, unless a mistake was made by the surveyor in 1566 and Spryng Wells Yarde was really east of the lane, it might have been opposite the Friary's holy well and its neighbouring springs.

---

5   Partly this must be down to East Anglia's geology and rainfall, meaning there are generally not as many springs here as e.g. in the west of the UK.

6   NHLE 1013095. Interestingly, there is a spring with a similar dedication, called the 'Lady-well', associated with the remains of another Carmelite friary: Appleby (Cumbria) (O'Sullivan, *In the Company of Preachers*, p.32).

7   Morris, *Churches in the Landscape* (London 1989), quoted in Whyte, *Inhabiting the Landscape*, p.41.

8   Heywood, 'Existing Remains Including Friary Cottage and Our Lady's Well', p.97.

There is evidence of English recusants and even foreign Catholic pilgrims continuing to visit holy wells into the seventeenth century in places all over the British Isles, even if any built structures associated with them had long been destroyed.[9] Other Catholics went further, and used holy wells for baptisms.[10] If these kinds of things happened at Burnham Norton, they would have been clandestine. They would have only left a written record if seen and acted upon by the authorities.

The Friary spring is next mentioned in a 1903 manuscript, written by an anonymous author about his recollections of the Burnhams in the 1840s.[11] The writer recounts how it was a 'place of resort' for local people. He gives the following vivid description: '... there was a half-circle cut out of a hill of rising ground ... faced with rock ... from it in all parts ran little rills of pure water which formed themselves into a narrow, shallow stream with the pebbles clean and bright beneath.' Nearby was the main spring itself, enclosed by 'four large stones sunk in the ground to form a square, in which a large pail might be dipped in and filled with beautiful clear water.' The spot is marked on the first edition 25 inch OS map (1887) as 'Our Lady's Well'. In 1963, the present author's grandmother recorded her childhood memories of the village from about 1915: 'I wonder how many of the school children to-day know of the "Wishing Well" ... many times in the Summer when coming home from school we would stop and have a drink and the water was always so clear and cold; I often wonder if all our wishes were fulfilled'.[12] More recently, the holy well was featured in Kevin Crossley-Holland's beautiful poem *Jesus of Norton*, later set to music and retitled *The Wellspring*.[13]

The spring is still identified by many of the older residents of the district as a wishing well or holy well. Despite its secularisation after 1538, a cultural memory of its spiritual importance to the Carmelites seems to be still preserved today.

9   Walsham, *Reformation of the Landscape*, pp.167, 171, 174.
10   Walsham, *Reformation of the Landscape*, p.180.
11   Anon., 'Burnham Market as I Remember It', p.17.
12   Francis, 'Norton News', May 1963 entry.
13   Crossley-Holland, *Swarm and Honeycomb*, item III.

Appendix 2 Prisoners-of-war camp

In the early twentieth century, global circumstances unimaginable to those whose lives had been in entangled with the history of the Friary both before and after its dissolution gave rise to a brief but extraordinary episode in the site's story: in 1917 it became a camp for German prisoners of war (POWs).[1] Why or how the Friary was selected as the location of a POW camp is unclear, and the exact position of the camp structures within the friary precinct is unknown.[2]

Numbers of German POWs held in Britain grew throughout the Great War and by 1916 the Prisoners of War Employment Committee was set up to organise work for enemy combatants (excluding officers). Edward Milligen Beloe (1871–1932) of King's Lynn, solicitor, antiquary and a leading light of the Norfolk & Norwich Archaeological Society, was assigned the post of camp commandant. Beloe had military experience in the 5th Battalion of the Norfolk Regiment, appearing on the Retired List in 1914 and later serving as Captain in the Royal Defence Corps (RDC).[3] The latter was formed in 1916 to defend important strategic locations in the UK, subsequently being used to guard POW camps.

One aspect of these camps was the need to provide POWs with a means of making small purchases, without furnishing them with money that would be useful after escaping. This problem was solved by using POW camp tokens. For camps on British soil, the tokens were typically uniface sixpence, shilling and higher denomination pieces, made from zinc-plated steel to a generic design. They were

[1] Francis, *Burnham Norton*, p.34.
[2] It was hoped that information on the POW camp might be discovered in the Walpole papers at the Norfolk Record Office in NRO WLP 8/114, 1060X5 about war-time use of Walpole (the owners of the site during WWI) land, but these papers are silent on Burnham Norton.
[3] *The London Gazette* 24 November 1908, p.8703; *ibid.* 13 January 1914, p.335; Anon., *Record of Service of Solicitors 1914–1919*, p.39.

Plate 22. A token from Burnham Norton
Prisoners-of-war camp. © The author.

utilitarian, and worlds apart from the penny tokens created by Beloe
for Burnham Norton (Plate 22). His were bi-faced, struck not only
in tin but also in bronze, contrary to DORA (Defence of the Realm
Act) regulations.[4] They display the cleverly encrypted date of 1917,
coded by enlarged capitals in the wording on the token's obverse, and
the legend '*CAPTIVORUM CUSTOS CAPTIVUS*' translating as 'the
prisoners' guard is himself a prisoner'. It may seem odd that a swastika
symbol also appears on the token, but this is an ancient symbol for
peace and good fortune, still retaining this meaning in 1917, and not
today's connotations. A surviving POW camp plate (Plate 23) also
has one of Beloe's encrypted dates, again for 1917, and was made by
the Staffordshire firm of Bishop & Stonier.[5] Notice the interesting
word '*LAAGER*' in the plate's inscription; this is an Afrikaans term
and originally meant a defensive position made by a circle of wagons.[6]

---

4   Beloe also had a special medal struck for his wife. A pencil rubbing, and
    a description, of it is given by Malcolm ('British First World War POW
    Tokens', Plate 5, no. 10).
5   Pottery mark identified in Godden, *Encyclopaedia of Pottery Marks*, p.76.
6   This may have reflected two things. First, that recollections of the Boer
    War (1899–1902) were still fresh. Second, that this war had also seen the

PRISONERS OF VVAR LAAGER
BVRNHAM NORTON Nᴿ KINGS LYNN
CO NORFOLK ᶠD ᵦELOE CAPN

Plate 23. A plate made for the Prisoners-of-war camp. © The author.

The surviving camp bell has similar lettering to the plate and is thus
dated 1917. Bespoke designs and a considerable level of investment
were made in items to be used at the Burnham Norton camp. This
may imply that the camp was not intended as merely a temporary
site for the POWs, but that there was an expectation that it would
remain in use throughout the war.

It is not certain exactly when in 1917 the camp became opera-
tional. However, by November that year the 'Commandant and RDC
Guard of the Burnham Norton P.W. camp' were providing a monthly
donation of £1 towards a relief fund for Norfolk Regiment POWs
overseas.[7] This was a generous sum compared with other donors, and
Burnham Norton was the only POW camp on the donors' list. A
piece in the local church magazine, from the same month, invites
readers to speculate what the friars might have thought about their

---

origination of what were known as concentration camps, comprising
tents.

7   *Eastern Daily Press* 1 November 1917, p.2; *ibid.* 2 November 1917, p.4.

precinct's use as a POW camp, particularly of the 'armed men set to guard' the prisoners, and of the former's 'tramping to and fro, on Sentry-go …'.[8]

In 2002, brief records were made based on interviews with the late Frederick Raven of Burnham Norton, when the former was in his late eighties.[9] His father was one of the one Parish Constables who helped at the camp. These revealed that the camp itself consisted of tents in a square, fenced compound.[10] The location of this compound is now forgotten, but it is likely to have been at the western end of the precinct, the area of highest relief at the site, yet away from the undulating ground of the buried foundations near the gatehouse.

The POWs were remembered clearing the River Burn, 'fying-out' (cleaning) the dykes on local marshes and helping at harvest time, therefore substituting for the labour of local men fighting abroad. When the POWs were working at the river, apparently they used to catch eels and store them in a hole in the soil covered by a lid made of a piece of turf, for cooking later. After the war, one local farmer contested the charges for work to his dykes and the court case was reported in the local newspaper in 1919.[11] A gang of sixteen POWs had been supervised by a local marshman and had worked for 2,786 hours on the task. Although Beloe testified that 'he had on occasion punished some of them [the POWs] for slackness in work', the consensus of most of the witnesses was that the German captives had worked well.

It is said that one of the prisoners died and was buried with full military honours at Burnham Ulph church and rifles were fired over the church as a mark of respect. Another of the prisoners (possibly a

---

8   Quoted by Sabin, 'Bare Ruin'd Choirs: The Carmelite Friary at Burnham Norton', pp.9–10.

9   Francis, *Burnham Norton*, p.34. The other Parish Constable helping at the POW camp was John William Bray Smith, the author's great-grandfather, who died in 1940. The POWs made wooden toys (now lost) for the author's grandfather, who would have been about 7 at the time.

10 As was the case at Euston in Suffolk (SRO, Bury St. Edmunds Branch, K997/39/5, German prisoners of war, photograph: eleven men 'By their tent at Euston' *c.*1917). There are no known photographs connected with the Burnham Norton camp.

11 *Eastern Daily Press* 7 May 1919, p.9.

Mr Essler) married a local girl. However, the present author can find no documentary evidence for this.

We know none of the Burnham Norton camp POWs' names. British records complied by the Prisoners of War Information Bureau were largely lost after enemy action in 1940; likewise German records of the Deutsche Dienststelle 'WASt' were destroyed by bombing in 1945.[12] The records of the International Commission of the Red Cross are not currently classified in a way which allows searching by a POW camp's name or location.[13]

Perhaps due to a lack of space to expand at the Friary, or the guards' (and prisoners') dislike of sleeping under canvas, the POW camp was re-located indoors to the former maltings in Station Road, Burnham Market (TF 83270 41996), and so departed from the story of the Friary. The date of the move is uncertain, but the POWs were housed in the new camp at Burnham Market by Christmas 1918.[14] Thus ended one of the strangest episodes in the history of the site at Burnham Norton.

---

[12] http://www.nationarchives.gov.uk; Irit Thorow (Deutsche Dienststelle 'WASt') pers. comm., 2 May 2018.

[13] Fania Khan (International Commission for the Red Cross) pers. comm., 8 May 2018.

[14] POW camp Christmas card, NMS KILLM 1982.15. The wording on the POW camp Christmas card shows that by 1918, Beloe also controlled POW camps at Gayton, Snettisham, Docking and Houghton. An additional Burnham Market camp Christmas card, in German, also survives (NMS KILLM 1973.43.20). It shows a sketch labelled '*DIE LAGERGLOKE WEINACHTEN 1918*' ('the Camp-bell Christmas 1918'). The Burnham Market camp remained in use until at least 1919, when it was one of several inspected by Dr A. de Sturler and Monsieur R. de Sturler of the Swiss Legation (TNA FO 383/507).

Appendix 3 Stone survey results

This Appendix sets out the detailed results of a survey of re-used limestone in Burnham Norton, the methodology for which is set out on pages 87–8. The site number refers to the numbering system used for this survey, and not house numbers in the residential properties' addresses. The results detail the number of identified limestone pieces recorded, and each wall's construction materials are in parentheses. See also Figs. 6 & 7.

1   Pound Cottage, Friars Lane (TF 83735 42888)
Extant in 1825.
(a) House: N gable, 16 pieces, including a carved corbel/impost (mixed materials); E wall, 2 (largely brick); S wall, 1 (mixed materials); W wall, 31 (mixed materials).
(b) Roadside garden wall N face, 8 (mixed materials).

2   Keeper's Cottage, Main Road (TF 82941 43569)
Built between c.1840 & 1886.
N & S gables, none (random clunch, some brick headers); E wall unsurveyed; W wall, none (brick).

3   The Pightle roadside wall, Norton Street (TF 82980 43562 to TF 82998 43514)
South of next entry. More than half the wall covered in ivy.
E face, 1 (mixed materials).

4   46 Norton Street (TF 82974 43571)
Extant in 1825; C17th/18th in style.
N & S gables, none (coursed clunch); E wall, none (coursed, knapped & galleted flint); W wall unsurveyed.

5   44 Norton Street (TF 82968 43582)
Built between c.1840 & 1886; terracotta digits, '1924', and terracotta Leicester cypher on E gable.

N & E walls, none (brick); S wall, 1 (mixed materials); W gable unsurveyed.

6   42 Norton Street (TF 82959 43612)
Built between 1825 & c.1840; semi-detached with next entry.
N wall unsurveyed; E gable, none (coursed clunch); S wall, 4 (mixed materials).

7   40 Norton Street (TF 82948 43605)
Built between 1825 & c.1840; semi-detached with previous entry.
N wall unsurveyed; W & S walls, none (brick).

8   Norton Hall, 34 Norton Street (grid references below)
House, C17th, listed Grade II (no. 1238879); principal house in the village.
(a) House (TF 82922 43763): N gable, unknown (rendered); E wall, none (mixed materials); S gable, none (brick); W wall, none (brick); S wing N wall, 1.
(b) Coach house & stables (TF 82891 43734): N wall, 6 (mixed materials); E gable, 2 (mixed materials); S & W walls, none (brick).
(c) Rear courtyard garden (TF 82891 43734): N wall, none (mixed materials); W wall, E face, 5 (mixed materials).
(d) Roadside garden wall (TF 82944 43781 to approximately TF 82949 43688) E face, 32 (mixed materials).
(e) W garden wall beside rear drive (TF 82915 43727 to approximately TF 82910 43669) W face, none (mixed materials).
(f) Semi-circular garden feature (approximately TF 82949 43628), 8.

9   Home Close roadside wall, Norton Street (TF 82954 43777 to approximately TF 82949 43692)
Opposite Norton Hall.
W face, 13 including 3 chamfered blocks, possibly parts of door jambs or window frames (mixed materials).

10   Wagon Shed, Norton Street (TF 82957 43798)
Extant in 1825; part of Norton Hall Farm; PO letterbox in gable wall.
N wall, 2 (mainly clunch); E gable, none (C20th brick); open-fronted on S; W gable, 1 (mixed materials).

11   Former Hospital Box, Norton Street (TF 82962 43807)
Terracotta digits, '1884', on gable; former Norton Hall Farm building; abuts No. 35's garden.
N wall, none (mixed materials); W gable, 1 (mixed materials); remainder unsurveyed.

12   Horse Yard, Norton Street (TF 82925 43791)
Extant in 1825; part of Norton Hall Farm; abuts N side of Norton Hall's gardens.
(a) Stables & harness room on N of yard: N & W walls unsurveyed; E gable, none; S wall, 4 (both mainly clunch).
(b) Horse Yard W wall E face, none (mixed materials).
(c) Roadside wall, E face 1 (mixed materials).
(d) Horse Yard S wall N face, 66 including 2 large window mullion segments, 2 smaller mullions and 7 possible cloister mullion pieces (mixed materials).

13   35 Norton Street (TF 82947 43826)
Extant in 1825; C17th/C18th in style.
(a) House: N wall, none; E gable, none (C20th brick); S wall, none; W gable, none (mixed materials).
(b) Stub wall from W gable, N face, 1 (mixed materials).
(c) Roadside wall W face, 2 (mixed materials).

14   Old Bullock Box, 1 Blacksmith's Lane (TF 82924 43830)
Built between 1825 & c.1840; former Norton Hall Farm building.
N wall, none; E wall, 2; W gable, none (all mixed materials); courtyard-facing walls modern.

15   Coal Yard Barn, 2 Blacksmith's Lane (TF 82911 43857)
N range extant in 1825; remainder built between 1840 & 1886; graffito on E wall, 'V R 1842'; former Norton Hall Farm building.
(a) House: N wall unsurveyed; E wall, 10 including 1 large window mullion segment, 1 chamfered block possibly from a door jamb or window frame, and 1 very damaged block that might be from a shuttered opening; S gable, 6 (all mixed materials); courtyard-facing walls modern.
(b) Roadside courtyard wall S face, none (mixed materials).

16 Trowland Barn, 3 Blacksmith's Lane (TF 82896 43810)

Built between c.1840 & 1886 (same design as Great Farm Barn); semi-detached with next entry (part of same original barn); former Norton Hall Farm building.

N wall, 1 (mixed materials); remainder unsurveyed.

17 Norton Great Barn, 5 Blacksmith's Lane (TF 82883 43802)

Built between c.1840 & 1886 (same design as Great Farm Barn); semi-detached with previous entry (part of same original barn); former Norton Hall Farm building.

N wall, none (mixed materials); W gable, none (mixed materials); remainder unsurveyed.

18 Norton Barn, 31 Norton Street (TF 82973 43839)

N range extant in 1825; E range extant in 1825, then lost and re-built between 1886 & 1904; former Norton Hall Farm building; some rebuilding during conversion 1988–1990.

(a) N range: N wall, 1 in possible repair (coursed clunch on coursed flint plinth); E gable, none (brick); S wall, 1 large block in foundations; W gable, none (coursed clunch on coursed flint plinth).

(b) E range (mixed materials): E wall, 2; S gable, 1; W wall, modern timber.

(c) Wall between barn and road N face, 1 (mixed materials, some coursed clunch).

19 Norton South Barn, 33 Norton Street (TF 82977 43811)

Extant in 1825; former Norton Hall Farm building.

N wall, 3; E gable, none; S wall, 1 piece (all mixed materials).

20 Bottom Meadow roadside wall, Norton Street (TF 82907 43894 to TF 82935 43835)

Opposite Hill Stile House.

W face, 2 (mixed materials).

21 Hill Stile House roadside wall, 26 Norton Street (TF 82895 43899 to TF 82912 43863)

E face, 3 (mixed materials).

22 Meg's Cottage garden walls, 23 Norton Street (grid references below)
Site of two semi-detached houses and outbuildings in 1825; W house demolished by c.1840; E house demolished, new dwelling built on footprint (using new materials) and new N garden wall reconstructed with rubble from old garden wall and ruined pigsty c.1997/8.
(a) N garden wall (TF 82926 43907 to TF 82954 43923) S face, 28 (mixed materials).
(b) S garden wall (TF 82907 43895 to TF 82940 43904) N face, 3 (mixed materials).

23 Creek Cottage outbuilding and adjoining roadside wall, 24 Norton Street (TF 82891 43905)
Site of farmhouse and other buildings in 1825, largely demolished by 1886 leaving current outbuilding.
(a) Outbuilding (mixed materials): N gable, 1; E wall, 1; S gable, none; W wall, 1.
(b) Roadside garden wall E face, 4 (mixed materials).

24 Prince of Wales House, 21 Norton Street (TF 82900 43926)
House, C17th or earlier, listed Grade II (no. 1239089); outbuildings extant in 1825.
(a) House: N wall, 4 in blocked doorways (coursed clunch rubble); E gable, none (clunch and Victorian reconstruction in brick); S wall, 1 in possible repair (coursed clunch rubble); W gable, none (1930s rendered brick). Two Collyweston-type slates (a type of limestone 'slate' quarried in Northamptonshire) were found in the roof during works in 2002/3.
(b) Barn: N wall, none (mainly clunch); E gable, 1 (mixed materials); S wall, 3 in later hightening to wall (mixed materials).
(c) Wash-house: W wall, 3 (mixed materials); S gable, none (C20th brick).
(d) Garden wall N face, 1 (mixed materials).

25 Sea Peeps outbuilding and garden walls, 19 Norton Street (grid references below)

Ex Prince of Wales House land; outbuilding (former stables) extant c.1840; N garden wall C18th;[1] *roadside wall reconstructed in 1980s with rubble from previous wall.*

(a) Outbuilding (TF 82900 43952) (mixed materials throughout): N wall, 2; E gable, 1; S wall, 1; W gable, none.

(b) N garden wall (TF 82890 43949) N face, none (mixed materials, S face contains bee boles, i.e. niches built in a wall to protect straw hives over winter).

(c) Roadside wall (TF 82888 43931) W face, 1 (mixed materials). A Collyweston-type slate was discovered in the rubble of this wall during reconstruction.

26 The Step garden walls, 14 Norton Street (grid references below)

Near site of several cottages extant in 1825, demolished between 1886 & 1904. N part of roadside wall probably Victorian, rebuilt using old materials, 2008.

(a) Remains of E–W wall in garden (TF 82825 43952), 2 loose pieces.

(b) N–S internal garden wall (TF 82829 43961) W face, 3 (mixed materials).

(c) N section of roadside wall (TF 82860 43974), 1 (mixed materials).

27 Paradise Row, 11–17 Norton Street (TF 82879 43985)

Extant in 1825; modern extension on E end; S part of the roadside wall demolished in 2015 to make a new entrance.

(a) Row of cottages: N wall, 1 (mixed materials); E gable covered by modern extension; S wall, none (brick); W gable, 4 (mixed materials).

(b) Roadside garden wall W face, 25 (mixed materials). The demolished section was also rich in limestone, judging by the rubble that has been saved for another project.

28 Samphire Cottage roadside wall, 12 Norton Street (TF 82855 43982)

Close to site of several small cottages extant in 1825, demolished between 1886 & 1904.

E face, 1 (mixed materials).

---

[1] International Bee Research Association (IBRA) bee boles register.

29 Lodge Cottage, 7 Norton Street (TF 82863 44001)
Extant in 1825; C17th/C18th in style.
(a) House: N wall, 1 in plinth (coursed clunch on coursed flint plinth); E gable, none (modern reconstruction); S wall none (mostly coursed clunch); W gable, none (coursed flint pebbles).
(b) Roadside garden wall W face, 1 in blocked former gateway (mixed materials).

30 The Dunlins, 10 Norton Street (TF 82841 44008)
Extant in 1825.
N gable, unknown (rendered); E wall, 8 (mixed materials including many glacial erratics); S gable, none (mixed materials); W wall unsurveyed.

31 Norton Cottage, 6a & b Norton Street (grid references below)
Extant in 1825; date stone, '1859' or '1869'.
(a) House (TF 82788 44053): N wall unsurveyed; S wall, 1 (mainly chalk and glacial erratics); E wall, ? (rendered); W wall obscured by modern extension.
(b) Garage (TF 82830 44019): N gable, 1; E wall, none (timber); W wall, 1 (mixed materials).

32 Marsh Gate, 4 Norton Street (TF 82815 44058)
Extant in 1825; date stone, '1727'.
(a) House: N wall, 2 (mixed materials); E & S walls, none (brick); W gable & S extension unsurveyed.
(b) Roadside wall to N of house, E face, 3 (mixed materials).

33 The Lodge garden walls, 3 Norton Street (grid references below)
The site of cottages and pightles in 1825.
(a) Tennis court wall (TF 82851 44117) E face, 1 large block with a groove (mixed materials).
(b) Wall near house (TF 82870 44076), 1 in standing section and 1 in rubble (wall being partially reconstructed when surveyed).

34 Stable Flat, 1 Norton Street (TF 82865 44119)
Built between c.1840 & 1886.
N wall, 3; E gable obscured by later extension; S wall, 2; W gable, 5 (all mixed materials).

35 Corner Cottage roadside walls, 1 Marsh Lane (grid references below)

E roadside wall incorporates part of gable of cottages extant between 1825 & 1886.

(a) N garden wall (TF 82788 44147 to TF 82817 44139) N face, 2 (lower part coursed, galleted flint cobbles, upper part mixed materials, perhaps once a high-status structure).

(b) E garden wall (TF 82817 44139 to TF 82818 44097) E face, 13 (mixed materials).

36 St Antony's Cottage roadside wall, 3 Marsh Lane (TF 82716 44149 to TF 82746 44153)

N face, 1 (mixed materials).

37 Trackside wall near Marsh Farm, Marsh Lane (TF 82711 44292 to TF 82718 44201)

Gappy and semi-derelict.

E face, 3 (mixed materials).

38 Marsh Farm House, 6 Marsh Lane (grid references below)

Extant in 1825 and possibly dating to the C16th; site of former staithe cut off from the sea in 1822 by reclamation works.

(a) House (TF 82694 44324): N wall near door, 4; remainder, none (brick, render, flint or modern extension).

(b) N garden wall (TF 82705 44330) N face, 1 (mixed materials).

(c) SW garden wall (TF 82678 44318) S face, 21 (mixed materials).

39 East Barn, 4 Marsh Lane (TF 82704 44345)

Built between 1825 & c.1840, perhaps using demolition materials from possible former maltings to S of farmhouse and extant in 1825; part of Marsh Farm.

(a) Main range: N wall, none (partly obscured by N range); S wall, 1 (mainly clunch and brick); E wall, 47 including three mullion sections, and an octagonal block (mainly clunch and brick); W wall, 1 (mixed materials).

(b) N range: N wall, 60 (large areas comprise only limestone, the rest, mainly clunch and brick), also one worked, segment-shaped, grey, fine textured stone; S wall, none (mixed materials); E wall, 31 (mainly clunch and brick).

(c) Infill from demolished section of wall, 1 piece of window tracery from an arched window, and several moulded bricks from mullioned windows.

(d) As reported by owner: loose in garden, 20–30 voussoirs with hollow chamfers; indoors a re-used limestone doorway (jambs only, no head) with splayed dressings.

40 North Barn, 2 Marsh Lane (TF 82681 44351)
Comments same as for East Barn.

(a) House: N wall, 76 (large areas comprise only limestone, the rest, mainly clunch and brick); S wall, none (largely covered by modern extension); W wall, 6 (mixed materials).

(b) Garden wall N face, 8 (mixed materials).

41 Cosy Cottage, 5 Marsh Lane (TF 82681 44351)
Extant in 1825; C17th/C18th in style.

(a) House: N wall, 5 in possible repairs (mostly coursed clunch with area of coursed flint cobbles); E gable, none (C20th brick); S wall, none; W gable, none.

(b) Garden wall N & W faces, 5 (mixed materials).

42 Trowland Cottage, 8 Marsh Lane (TF 82655 44177)
N range extant in 1825; C17th/C18th in style; E range is modern.
Old range: N wall, 1 (mixed materials); original E gable covered by modern extension; original S wall, none (heavily altered recently); old range W gable, none (modern reconstruction).

43 Denning, 7 Marsh Lane (TF 82646 44137)
Extant in 1825; C17th/18th in style.
N wall, 3 in blocked former door (mostly coursed clunch); remainder unsurveyed.

44 Lechmere, 9 Marsh Lane (TF 82604 44134)
Extant in 1825; E extension built between 1904 & 1939.
N wall original section, 6 (mixed materials); N wall of later extension, none; remainder unsurveyed.

45   Bradmere House, Main Road (TF 82205 44011)
Extant c.1840.
(a) House: all elevations, none (clunch on brick plinth, some walls rebuilt *c*.2011).
(b) Dry-stone retaining wall to N, 6 (mixed materials).

46   Great Farm Barn, formerly called Field Barn[2] (TF 81414 43157)
Built between c.1840 & 1886 (same design as Trowland & Norton Great Barns); former Norton Hall Farm building.
Main barn: all elevations, none (clunch and brick, with some vitrified bricks in the infill). Other ranges rebuilt within the last ten years.

---

[2]   The postal address is incorrectly now Burnham Deepdale, but the barn is within Burnham Norton parish.

Bibliography

MANUSCRIPTS AND ARTWORKS

British Library (BL), London

MS Add. 6744. Fol. 39 'Sketch, in pen and ink, of the ruins of Burnham Norton Priory; drawn in 1769, by the Rev. Thomas Kerrich.'
MS Add. 6759. Fol. 6, 7, 11–18. Drawings by Rev. Thomas Kerrich.

Cornwall Record Office (CRO; Kresen Kernow), Redruth, Cornwall

'Records of Fortescue family and Boconnoc Estate.'
    F/4/177/9 'Copy conveyance, site of 'late dissolved howse or pryery of Fryer Carnellette in Burnham Norton' Norfolk 14 Jas I.'

Holkham Hall Archives, Holkham, Norfolk

'Conveyance between the Rt Hon. Robert Horace, Earl of Orford and the Rt Hon. Thomas William, Earl of Leicester. 8 June 1922.' Available online at: http://www.burnhamoveryharbour.com/Resources/ Conveyance%20of%20burnham%20estate%208%20june%201922.pdf

Norfolk Museums Services (NMS), King's Lynn Museums, King's Lynn, Norfolk

KILLM: 1973.43.20 'B/w printed card (card).'
KILLM: 1982.15 'Yuletide card (card).'

Norfolk Museums Services (NMS), Norwich Castle Museum, Norwich, Norfolk

NWHCM: 1951.235.702.B6 'Burnham Norton Gateway (drawing).'
NWHCM: 1951.235.702.B7 'Burnham Norton Church (drawing).'
NWHCM: 1954.138.Todd14.Gallow.27 'Burnham Norton Church (ruin) (drawing).'
NWHCM: 1954.138.Todd14.Gallow.30 'Ruins of the Carmelites Convent at Burnham Overy (print).'

Norfolk Record Office (NRO), Norwich, Norfolk

Norfolk County Quarter Sessions:

C/Sca 1/1 'Deeds of Bargain and Sale 10 Feb 1561 to 21 Feb 1579'
mm. 16–18 Bromfield and Pepys to Jenyson, 7 June 8 Eliz.
mm. 42–42d Pepys to Cobbs, 20 Dec 9 Eliz.

C/Sca 2/61/1 'An Act for Embanking, Draining, Inclosing, and
Improving Certain Salt Marshes and Waste Lands, within the
Parishes of Burnham Norton, Burnham Deepdale and Burnham
Overy, in the County of Norfolk. 2 Geo IV Sess. 1821 (Royal
Assent, 19 April 1821).'

C/Sca 2/62 'Burnham Deepdale, Norton and Overy [Map: Burnham
Salt Marshes, 1819 (certified 1821)].'

Norwich Diocesan Archives:

DN/TA 'Diocese of Norwich: Tithe Maps and Apportionments'
229 'Burnham Norton Tithe Map (no date) and Apportionment, 1840.'
349 'Burnham Overy Tithe Map and Apportionment, 1840.'
358 'Burnham Sutton Tithe Map, 1840; Apportionment, 1841.'
386 'Burnham Westgate alias Burnham Market Tithe Map, 1837,
and Apportionment, 1841.'

Family Papers and Collections:

Hare 'Hare of Stow Bardolph Collection'
598, 187X6 'Charter: Feoffment to Uses. John Fyncham of Fyncham
son and heir of John Fyncham eldest son of John Fyncham late
of Fyncham decd. to Thomas Thorysby of Asshewekyng, Thomas
Dereham, jun., William Skypwith, jun., Humphrey Karbell of
Wygenhale St Mary, jun., Simon Fyncham son of John Fyncham
of Outewell, Gilbert Bachecroft, clerk, and John Prent. 1 Dec 1526.'

Minor Collections:

'Survey of Burnham manors'
MC 1830/1, 852X7 'Norfolk Estates: a Survey and Valuation of the
Manors of Burnham Lexham and Burnham Polstead Hall and
of several other Estates in the parishes of Burnham Westgate,
Burnham Norton, Burnham Ulph, Burnham Overy, Burnham
Thorpe, Burnham Sutton and Snettisham, and the advowsons
of the rectories of Burnham Westgate and Burnham Deepdale,
the joint property of the late Mrs Mary Smith and the late Ann
Dowager Baroness Camelford. *c.*1796.'

'Lombard of Burnham Estate Papers'
MC 567/1–22, 778X4 'Receipted bills paid by Robert Discipline
for Peter Lombard at Burnham Thorpe.'

Norwich Public Library Manuscript Collection:

MS 18809, 100X2 'Manor of Burnham Thorpe with the members. Extract from Court Roll. Admission of Charles Douglass Smith on the death of Mary Smith, his mother. 10 Dec 1805.'

MS 3254, 4B1 'Writ of praecipimus addressed to the escheator of Norfolk to give seizin to Thomas Jenyson, son and heir of Robert Jenyson, gent., decd, of premises settled on him by the will of the said Robert. 21 Nov 1583.'

WAL 'Walpole of Wolterton estate records'

119/1, 269X5 'Indenture: Release. (1) Elizabeth Overman of Wells next the Sea, widow. (2) John Bennington of Burnham Norton, yeoman. 11 Apr 1690.'

146/5, 270X2 'William Bennington of Massingham his affidavit of his estate in Burnham Norton and Westgate free from incumbrances. c.1746.'

820, 281X5 'Copy Final Concord. William Tindal, plaintiff. Thomas Savile, Esq., and Hugh Myddelton, gent., deforciants. 1674–5.'

876/1, 282X4 'Indenture: Settlement. (1) Sir Hugh Middleton late of Hackney (Midd.) and Dame Dorothea his wide. (2) Bartholomew Soame, citizen and goldsmith of London. (3) John Goldsmith of Middle Temple and another. Estate in Burnham Norton and Burnham St Andrew. 25 May 1689.'

876/3, 282X4 'Indenture of Bargain and Sale. (1) John Goldsmith of Middle Temple, Esq., and others. (2) John Smith of Thistleworth (Midd.), Esq. 7 May 1690.'

876/5, 282X4 'Indentures of Lease and Release. (1) Sir John Smith of Thistleworth (Midd.), Bt., and others. (2) Peter Lombard of Burnham Thorpe, Esq. 29–30 Apr 1723.'

900, 283X1 'Articles of agreement for purchase of manors lands tenements in Burnham Thorpe, Burnham Overy and Holkham … 28 Jun 1707.'

964/1, 284X1 'Indenture of Lease and Release of messuage malthouse and estate in Burnham Norton. Thomas Dewing to Charles Dewing. 16–17 Jun 1756.'

1083, 285X3 'Indenture: Covenant to levy a fine and deed to declare the uses thereof. (1) John Bensley of Burnham Westgate, yeoman, and Mary his wife. (2) Rt. Hon. Horatio Walpole of Woolterton, Esq. 23 Aug 1746.'

1162, 282X6 'Indenture: Deed of partition between Horatio Walpole, Esq. and Isaac Leheup, Esq. 9 May 1729.'

WLP 'Records of the Walpole Family of Wolterton (additional)'
    8/33, 1044X8 'Papers re. estate at Barningham, the Burnham estate, re. Wickmere tithes dispute and re. house and window tax. 1743–1759.'
    8/114, 1060X5 'Correspondence and other papers concerning camp and military use of land at Weybourne and Weybourne, Holkham, Burnham and Sheringham rifle ranges. 1915–1921.'
    10/7, 1039X5 'Plans for restoration of Burnham Priory gateway.'

The National Archives (TNA), London

'Court of Chancery: Six Clerks Office: Pleadings 1714 to 1758'
    C11/2666/32 'Short title: Smith v Richardson. Plaintiffs: Sir John Smith, carpenter of Isleworth, Middlesex and Bacon Hibgame, yeoman of Burnham Norton, Norfolk. Defendants: Clement Richardson, Thomas Mayle alias Thomas Male, John Bell senior, Margaret Alley alias Margaret Otley, William Bennington, John Fish, John Tilney, Robert Bell and John Bell junior. 1719–1739.'
'Chancery and Supreme Court of Judicature: Patent Rolls'
    C66/708 m. 32–3 Patent Roll 33 Henry VIII, Part 8, 25 May 1541. Lands and tenants granted to Cobham and Warner.
    C66/725 m. 16 Patent Roll 35 Henry VIII, Part 4, 21 February 1544. Lands and tenants granted to Calthorpe.
    C66/784 m. 4 Patent Roll 37 Henry VIII, Part 17, 8 November 1545. Lands and tenants granted to Blennerhasset.
    C66/984 m. 6 Patent Roll 4 Elizabeth I, Part 9, 24 November 1561. Lands and tenants granted to Bromefelde and Pepes.
    C66/1063 m. 16 Patent Roll 12 Elizabeth I, Part 3, 9 February 1570. Lands and tenants granted to Mynne and Hall.
    C66/1125 m. 30 Patent Roll 17 Elizabeth I, Part 3, 22 September 1575. Lands and tenants granted to Herbert & Palmer.
    C66/1155 m. 12 Patent Roll 19 Elizabeth I, Part 5, 28 November 1576. Lands and tenants granted to Grymeston.
'Foreign Office: Prisoners of War and Aliens Department: General Correspondence from 1906'
    FO 383/507 'Reports on visits of inspection to prisoner of war camps in the UK by Dr A de Sturler and Monsieur R de Sturler of the Swiss Legation during April and May 1919.'
'Prerogative Court of Canterbury and related Probate Jurisdictions: Will Registers'
    PROB 11/35/71 'Will of Sir Philip Calthorpe of Erwarton, Suffolk. 15 February 1552.'

PROB 11/343/488 'Will of John Soame, Bachelor of Burnham Market, Norfolk. 13 December 1673.'

PROB 11/346/14 'Sentence of John Soame, Bachelor of Burnham Market, Norfolk. 28 February 1674.'

PROB 11/409/175 'Will of John Harris of Lupset Hall, Yorkshire. 09 April 1692.'

'Ministers' and Receivers' Accounts. Norfolk: Monastic Possessions etc.'

SC 6/HENVIII/2632 (22 April 1539 – 21 April 1541) rot. 54d–55a

SC 6/HENVIII/2633 (22 April 1540 – 21 April 1542) rot. 49

SC 6/HENVIII/2634 (22 April 1541 – 21 April 1543) rot. 38d

SC 6/HENVIII/2635 (22 April 1542 – 21 April 1544) rot. 30d

SC 6/HENVIII/7438 (22 April 1539 – 21 April 1541) rot. 9

SC 6/HENVIII/7439 (22 April 1540 – 21 April 1542) rot. 13

SC 6/HENVIII/7440 (22 April 1543 – 21 April 1545) rot. 8d

SC 6/HENVIII/7441 (22 April 1545 – 21 April 1547) rot. 10

'Letters and papers published in Letters and Papers … of the reign of Henry VIII, vol. XIII'

SP 1/132 fol. 101 Letter from Jane Calthorpe, 17 May 1538.

'Exchequer: King's Remembrancer: Miscellanea relating to the Dissolution of the Monasteries and to the General Surveyors (formerly State Papers Henry VIII Suppression Papers)'

SP 5/4/152 fol. 126 'Norf. and Suff. Friaries: memorandum giving reasons for preserving the following houses: Burnham Norton etc.'

'Court of Wards and Liveries: Deeds and Evidences'

WARD 2/34/132/1 'Quitclaim by Agnes, widow of John de Brunham, to Alice Gauge of the same, for 10s of silver, of a messuage in Burnham Norton (Brunham Norton), [Norfolk], near to Bradmere (Berdemere), with three acres of land. 31 Mar 1301.'

Private collections

'Burnham Inclosure Award 1826'. Copy held privately in the Burnhams (used here); there is also a copy at the Norfolk Record Office (see above): NRO C/Sca 2/60.

'A Burnham Norton Estate. Declaration [and map] by Mr William B. Lane. 23 February 1886.' Owned by the author.

Francis, H.L. 'Norton News', 1962–83. Owned by the author.

Friary Cottage photographs collection. Held by the owners of Friary Cottage.

Suffolk Record Office (SRO), Bury St Edmunds Branch, Suffolk

'Walton Burrell Archive'
   K997/39/5 'German prisoners of war, Euston, Suffolk'. *c.*1917.

*West Yorkshire Archive Service (WYAS), Calderdale, Halifax,
West Yorkshire*

'Muniments of Kirklees and the Armytage Family'
   KM/852 'Deeds relating to Hartshead, Clifton, etc.'

PUBLICATIONS

Alban, John, 'Benefactors Great and Small: Late Medieval Wills
   Relating to Burnham Norton Friary', in Brendan Chester-Kadwell
   (ed.) *Burnham Norton Friary: Perspectives on the Carmelites in Norfolk*
   (Norwich 2019) pp.155–74
Alexander, Jennifer S., 'Building Stone from the East Midlands Quarries:
   Sources, Transportation and Usage', *Medieval Archaeology*, 39 (1995)
   pp.107–35
Andrews, Frances, *The Other Friars: Carmelite, Augustinian, Sack and Pied
   Friars in the Middle Ages* (Woodbridge 2006)
Anon., 'Burnham Market as I Remember It Sixty Years Ago', in *Burnham
   Market Records and Recollections* (Burnham Market 1997) pp.7–20
——, *The English Baronetage*, vol. III(II) (London 1741)
——, *Record of Service of Solicitors and Articled Clerks with His Majesty's
   Forces 1914–1919* (London no date)
Banks, W.S., *Walks in Yorkshire: Wakefield and its Neighbourhood*
   (London 1871)
Barratt, Alexandra, *The Knowing of Woman's Kind in Childing*
   (Turnhout 2001)
Barringer, J.C. (ed.), *Bryant's Map of Norfolk in 1826* (Dereham 1998)
—— (ed.), *Faden's Map of Norfolk. First Printed in 1797* (Dereham 1989)
Baxter, Stephen B., *England's Rise to Greatness, 1660–1763* (Berkeley 1983)
Bliss, W.H., and Twemlow, J.A., *Calendar of Papal Registers Relating to
   Great Britain and Ireland*, vol. IV (1362–1414) (London 1902)
Blomefield, Francis, *An Essay Towards a Topographical History of the County
   of Norfolk*, vol. I (London 1805)
——, and Parkin, Charles, *Ibid.*, vol. VI (London 1807)
——, and ——, *Ibid.*, vol. VII (London 1807)
——, and ——, *Ibid.*, vol. IX (London 1808)

——, and ——, *Ibid.*, vol. X (London 1809)

Blunt, John Henry, Rev. *The Reformation of the Church of England: Its History, Principles and Results*, vol. I (London 1882)

Bramston, John, *The Autobiography of Sir John Bramston, K.B. of Skreens, in the Hundred of Chelmsford* (Camden Society, Old Series, 32; London 1845)

Bryant, T. Hugh, *The Churches of Norfolk: Hundred of Brothercross* (Norwich 1914)

Builder, The, vol. 16 (1858)

Bulwer, J., 'Hassett's House, Norwich', *Norfolk Archaeology*, VII (1872) pp.79–91

Burke, John, and Burke, John Bernard, *A Genealogical and Heraldic History of the Extinct and Dormant Baronetcies of England* (2nd edn., London 1844)

Caius, John (ed. John Venn), *Annals of Gonville and Caius* (Cambridge 1904)

Calendar of the Patent Rolls of Edward I (CPR Edw. I)
vol. III 1292–1301, edited by H.C. Maxwell Lyte (London 1895)

Calendar of the Patent Rolls of Edward III (CPR Edw. III)
vol. VIII 1348–1350, edited by H.C. Maxwell Lyte (London 1905)
vol. IX 1350–1354, edited by H.C. Maxwell Lyte (London 1907)

Calendar of the Patent Rolls of Henry III (CPR Hen. III)
vol. V 1258–1266, edited by H.C. Maxwell Lyte (London 1910)

Calendar of the Patent Rolls of Elizabeth I (CPR Eliz. I)
vol. II 1560–1563 (London 1948)
vol. V 1569–1572 (London 1966)
vol. VII 1575–1578 (London 1982)
vol. VIII 1578–1580 (London 1986)

Candler, Charles, 'On the Significance of some East Anglian Field-Names', *Norfolk Archaeology*, XXI (1891) pp.143–78

Carr-Calthrop, C.W., *Notes on the Families of Calthorpe and Calthrop in the Counties of Norfolk and Lincolnshire and Elsewhere* (3rd edn., London 1933)

Chester-Kadwell, Brendan, 'The Medieval Friary Site at Burnham Norton and its Landscape Context', in Brendan Chester-Kadwell (ed.) *Burnham Norton Friary: Perspectives on the Carmelites in Norfolk* (Norwich 2019) pp.45–68

Clark, James G., *The Dissolution of the Monasteries: A New History* (New Haven & London 2021)

Clarke, Helen, 'From Hermits of Mount Carmel to Whitefriars in England *c.*1200–50', in Brendan Chester-Kadwell (ed.) *Burnham Norton Friary: Perspectives on the Carmelites in Norfolk* (Norwich 2019) pp.102–25

——, Mate, Mavis E., Pearson, Sarah, and Parfitt, Keith, *Sandwich, the 'Completest Medieval Town in England': A Study of the Town and Port From its Origins to 1600* (Oxford 2010)

Copsey, Richard, O. Carm., 'The Medieval Carmelite Priory at Burnham Norton: A Chronology', in Brendan Chester-Kadwell (ed.), *Burnham Norton Friary: Perspectives on the Carmelites in Norfolk* (Norwich 2019) pp.213–47

Coxe, William, *Memoirs of Horatio Lord Walpole*, vol. II (3rd edn., London 1820)

Crossley-Holland, Kevin, *Swarm and Honeycomb* (Wells-next-the-Sea 1998)

Cushion, Brian, and Davison, Alan, 'Earthworks of Norfolk', *East Anglian Archaeology*, 104 (2003)

Debrett, John, *The Peerage of the United Kingdom of Great Britain and Ireland*, vol. I (London 1820)

Doggett, Nick, 'The Demolition and Conversion of Former Monastic Buildings in Post-Dissolution Hertfordshire', in Graham Keevil, Mick Aston & Teresa Hall (eds.) *Monastic Archaeology: Papers on the Study of Medieval Monasteries* (Oxford 2017) pp.165–74

Druery, J.H., 'The Erpingham House, St Martin's at Palace, Norwich', *Norfolk Archaeology*, VI (1864) pp.143–8

Drummond, Mary M., 'Walpole, Hon. Horatio (1752–1822), of Wolterton, Norf.', in Sir Lewis Namier & John Brooke (eds.) *The History of Parliament: the House of Commons 1754–1790* (London 1964), *sub. nom.*

Eastern Daily Press, 1 November 1917; 2 November 1917; 7 May 1919

Edwards, P.S., 'Perrot (Parret), John (1528/29–92), of Haroldston and Carew Castle, Pemb.', in S.T. Bindoff (ed.) *The History of Parliament: the House of Commons 1509–1558* (London 1982) *sub. nom.*

Emery, Giles, 'Results of Recent Archaeological Surveys of the Burnham Norton Site', in Brendan Chester-Kadwell (ed.) *Burnham Norton Friary: Perspectives on the Carmelites in Norfolk* (Norwich 2019) pp.69–84

Festing, Sally, *Fishermen: A Community Living from the Sea* (Newton Abbot 1977)

Francis, Sally, *Burnham Norton: One of the Seven Burnhams by the Sea* (Burnham Norton 2003)

——, *Clarky Bottoms and Small Hopes: An Atlas of Place-Names in the Burnhams, Norfolk* (Burnham Norton 2009)

Gallois, R.W., *Geology of the Country around King's Lynn and the Wash* (London 1994)

Gardiner, Mark, 'Twelfth-Century Timbers From Sixhills, Lincolnshire, and a Review of Medieval Stave Construction in England', *Vernacular Architecture* 52 (2021) pp.30–40

Godden, Geoffrey A., *Encyclopaedia of British Pottery and Porcelain Marks* (London 1991)

Greenwood, John Beswicke, *The Early Ecclesiastical History of Dewsbury* (London 1859)

Hart, Stephen, *Flint Flushwork: A Medieval Masonry Art* (Woodbridge 2008)

Healey, Robin, and Escott, Margaret, 'Walpole, Horatio, Lord Walpole (1783–1858), of Wolterton, Norf. and 11 Berkeley Square, Mdx.', in D.R. Fisher (ed.) *The History of Parliament: the House of Commons 1820–1832*, VII (London and New York 2009) *sub. nom.*

Hesse, Mary, 'Fields, Medieval Field Systems and Land Tenure in South Creake, Norfolk', *Norfolk Archaeology* 43 (1998) pp.79–97

——, 'Fields, Tracks and Boundaries in the Creakes, North Norfolk', *Norfolk Archaeology* 41 (1992) pp.305–24

Heywood, Stephen, 'The Existing Remains Including Friary Cottage and Our Lady's Well', in Brendan Chester-Kadwell (ed.) *Burnham Norton Friary: Perspectives on the Carmelites in Norfolk* (Norwich 2019) pp.85–99

Hofmann, T.M., 'Warner, Sir Edward (1511–65), of Polsteadhall and Plumstead, Norf.', in S.T. Bindoff (ed.) *The History of Parliament: the House of Commons 1509–1558* (London 1982) *sub. nom.*

Holder, Nick (ed.), *The Friaries of Medieval London: From Foundation to Dissolution* (Woodbridge 2017)

Hooton, Jonathon, 'Imagined Coastlines – Coastal Change at the Port of Burnham', in Brendan Chester-Kadwell (ed.) *Burnham Norton Friary: Perspectives on the Carmelites in Norfolk* (Norwich 2019) pp.2–20

Howard, Joseph Jackson, and Chester, Joseph Lemuel (eds.), *The Visitation of London Anno Domini 1633, 1634, and 1635* (Publications of the Harleian Society, vol. XV, London 1883)

J.H., 'Grimston, Edward (*c.*1508–1600), of Rishangles, Suff.', in P.W. Hasler (ed.) *The History of Parliament: the House of Commons 1558–1603* (London 1981) *sub. nom.*

Johnson, S.R., 'Southwell, alias Darcy, Richard (by 1531–1600), of Lincoln's Inn, London; Horsham St. Faith, Norf. and Gatton, Surr.', in S.T. Bindoff (ed.) *The History of Parliament: the House of Commons 1509–1558* (London 1982) *sub. nom.*

Jones, Graham, *Saints in the Landscape* (Stroud 2007)

Kelly, E.R., *The Post Office Directory of Cambridge, Norfolk and Suffolk* (London 1864)

Lablanc, Michael L. (ed.), *Literature Criticism from 1400 to 1800* (Boston 2003)

Lee-Warner, H.J., 'The Calthorps of Cockthorp', *Norfolk Archaeology*, IX (1881) pp.153–79

Lee-Warner, James, 'The Calthorpes of Burnham', *Norfolk Archaeology*, IX (1880) pp.1–19

Letters and Papers, Foreign and Domestic, of the Reign of Henry VIII (L&P Henry VIII)

    vol. I, edited by J.S. Brewer (London 1862)

    vol. XII(I), edited by J. Gairdner (London 1890)

    vol. XII(II), edited by J. Gairdner (London 1891)

    vol. XIII(I), edited by J. Gairdner (London, 1892)

    vol. XIII(II), edited by J. Gairdner (London 1893)

    vol. XIV(I), edited by J. Gairdner & R.H. Brodie (London 1894)

    vol. XVI, edited by J. Gairdner & R.H. Brodie (London 1898)

    vol. XVII, edited by J. Gairdner & R.H. Brodie (London 1900)

    vol. XVIII(II), edited by J. Gairdner & R.H. Brodie (London 1902)

    vol. XIX(I), edited by J. Gairdner & R.H. Brodie (London 1903)

    vol. XX(II), edited by J. Gairdner & R.H. Brodie (London 1907)

Little, A.G., 'Corrodies at the Carmelite Friary at Lynn', *Journal of Ecclesiastical History*, 9 (1958) pp.8–29

London Gazette, The, 24 November 1908; 13 January 1914

MacDonald, S., 'The Progress of the Early Threshing Machine', *Agricultural History Review*, 23 (1975) pp.63–77

Malcolm, John, 'British First World War POW Tokens', *Journal of the London Numismatic Club Newsletter*, VII (1985) pp.25–6

Marshall, George William (ed.), *The Visitations of the County of Nottingham in the Years 1569 and 1614* (Publications of the Harleian Society, vol. IV, London 1871)

Marshall, W., *The Rural Economy of Norfolk*, vol. I (London 1787)

Midmer, Roy, *English Medieval Monasteries (1066–1540): A Summary* (London 1979)

Mimardière, A.M., 'Soame, Sir Stephen (*c*.1544–1619), of London', in P.W. Hasler (ed.) *The History of Parliament: the House of Commons 1558–1603* (London 1981) *sub. nom.*

Montgomery-Massingberd, Hugh (ed.), *Burke's Irish Family Records* (London 1976)

Moore, C.N., *St Margaret's Church Burnham Norton, with Notes on its Rectors, the Carmelite Friary and Norton Village* (Privately published no date)

M.R.P., 'Palmer, Andrew (*c*.1544–1599), of Cheapside and St. Peter-le-Poor, London', in P.W. Hasler (ed.) *The History of Parliament: the House of Commons 1558–1603* (London 1981) *sub. nom.*

Norfolk Chronicle, 16 September 1843

Norfolk News, 8 May 1852

Norwich Mercury, 23 July 1864

O'Sullivan, Deirdre, 'Friars, Friaries and the Reformation: The Dissolution of the Midlands Friaries in 1538–39,' *Midland History*, 44 (2019) pp.190–204

——, *In the Company of Preachers: The Archaeology of Medieval Friaries in England and Wales* (Leicester 2013)

Parrinder, Steve, *The Lost Abbey of Eynsham* (Oxford 2019)

Percival, Sarah, and Williamson, Tom, 'Early Fields and Medieval Furlongs: Excavations at Creake Road, Burnham Sutton, Norfolk', *Landscapes*, 6 (2005) pp.1–17

Pevsner, Nikolaus, and Wilson, Bill, *The Buildings of England. Norfolk 1: Norwich and North-East* (London 2002)

——, and ——, *The Buildings of England. 2: North-West and South* (London 2002)

Pierssené, Andrew, 'Burnham Norton Friary', *Water Transport in Norfolk, Site Reference 9* [site card to accompany Norfolk Heritage booklet Water Transport in Norfolk] (Gressenhall *c.*1977)

Record Commission, *Valor Ecclesiasticus*, vol. III (London 1817)

Ribot, Felipe (trans. and ed. Copsey, Richard, O. Carm.), *The Ten Books on the Way of Life and Great Deeds of the Carmelites* (Faversham 2007)

Rintoul, M.C., *Dictionary of Real People and Places in Fiction* (New York & London 1993)

Rogerson, Andrew, 'The Burnhams from the Fifth to the Fourteenth Centuries', in Brendan Chester-Kadwell (ed.) *Burnham Norton Friary: Perspectives on the Carmelites in Norfolk* (Norwich 2019) pp.21–44

Rye, Walter (ed.), *The Visitacion of Norfolk* [1563, 1589, 1613] (Publications of the Harleian Society, vol. XXXII, London 1891)

Sabin, Veronica, 'Bare Ruin'd Choirs: The Carmelite Friary at Burnham Norton', in *Burnham Market Records and Recollections* (Burnham Market 1994) pp.1–10

Samuel, Mark, 'Architecture and Architectural Fragments of the London Friaries', in Nick Holder (ed.) *The Friaries of Medieval London: From Foundation to Dissolution* (Woodbridge 2017) pp.211–26

Sedgwick, R.R., 'Walpole, Horatio (1678–1757), of Wolterton, Norf.', in R. Sedgwick (ed.) *The History of Parliament: the House of Commons 1715–1754*, II (London 1970) *sub. nom.*

——, 'Walpole, Hon. Horatio (1723–1809)', in R. Sedgwick (ed.) *The History of Parliament: the House of Commons 1715–1754*, II (London 1970) *sub. nom.*

Sheppard, Lancelot C., *The English Carmelites* (London 1943)

Smith, Peter, 'Beyond the Sea Wall: The Case of the Fishermen of Burnham Marshes', *Norfolk Archaeology*, 46 (2014) pp.37–44

Spelman, H., *The History and Fate of Sacrilege* (2nd edn., London 1853)

Spindler, Erik, 'Between Sea and City: Portable Communities in Late Medieval London and Bruges,' in Matthew Davies & James A. Galloway (eds.) *London and Beyond: Essays in Honour of Derek Keene* (London 2012) pp.181–200

Swainson, Charles, *Provincial Names and Folk Lore of British Birds* (London 1885)

Swales, T.H., 'Opposition to the Suppression of the Norfolk Monasteries. Expressions of Discontent: the Walsingham Conspiracy', *Norfolk Archaeology*, XXXIII (1964) pp.254–65

——, 'The Redistribution of Monastic Lands in Norfolk at the Dissolution', *Norfolk Archaeology*, XXXIV (1966) pp.14–44

Taylor, Richard, *Index Monasticus* (London and Norwich 1821)

Taylor, Thomas, *The History of Wakefield, in the County of York: The Rectory Manor* (Wakefield 1886)

Thrush, A., 'Grimston, Sir Harbottle, 1st Bt. (c.1578–1648), of Bradfield Hall, Essex', in A. Thrush & J.P. Ferris (eds.) *The History of Parliament: the House of Commons 1604–1629* (Cambridge 2010) *sub. nom.*

Tingey, J.C., 'A Calendar of Deeds Enrolled Within the County of Norfolk', *Norfolk Archaeology*, XIII (1896) pp.33–92

Victoria County History (VCH) of Norfolk
    Page, W. (ed.), *A History of the County of Norfolk*, vol. II (London 1906)

Vinten, Lucy, 'Friaries in East Anglia', *Annual Bulletin of the Norfolk Archaeological & Historical Research Group*, 3 (1994) pp.43–5

Virgoe, Roger, 'Southwell, Richard (1502/3–64), of London and Wood Rising, Norf.', in S.T. Bindoff (ed.) *The History of Parliament: the House of Commons 1509–1558*, III (London 1982), *sub. nom.*

Walsham, Alexandra, *The Reformation of the Landscape: Religion, Identity, and Memory in Early Modern Britian and Ireland* (Oxford 2011)

Warburton, Eliot (ed.), *Memoirs of Horace Walpole and His Contemporaries*, vol. II (London 1852)

Wentworth, John, *A Complete System of Pleading*, vol. X (Dublin 1799)

Whitaker, Jane, *Raised from the Ruins: Monastic Houses after the Dissolution* (London 2021)

White, William, *History, Gazetteer and Directory of Norfolk* (London 1864)

Whyte, Nicola, *Inhabiting the Landscape: Place, Custom and Memory, 1500–1800* (Oxford 2009)

Williamson, Tom, 'The Landscape Contexts', in L. Hodges (ed.) *The Anglo-Saxon Cemetery in Foundry Field, Burnham, Norfolk* (forthcoming)

———, *The Origins of Norfolk* (Manchester 1993)

Woodward, Samuel, and Ewing, W.C., *The Norfolk Topographer's Manual: A Catalogue of the Books and Engravings Hitherto Published in Relation to the County* (London 1842)

Wright, John, 'Blakeney Carmelite Friary', *The Glaven Historian*, 17 (2020) pp.3–33

Young, Arthur, *General View of the Agriculture of Norfolk* ([1804]; reprinted Newton Abbot 1969)

ONLINE SOURCES AND GREY LITERATURE

Bescoby, David, 'Imagined Land: St Mary's Friary, Burnham Norton. Geophysical Survey. 14 April 2017.' https://www.norfarchtrust.org.uk/wp-content/uploads/2019/05/Burnham-Norton-geophys-2017-report.pdf Accessed: March 2021

Campbell, C., 'James Bulwer fonds.' National Gallery of Canada, 2012. https://www.gallery.ca/library/ngc146.html#a0 Accessed: 10 December 2019

Heaton, Michael John, 'Spolia Britannica: The Historical Use of Salvaged Building Materials in Britain' (M.Phil. Thesis, Bath 2016)

Heywood, Stephen, and Rogerson, Andrew, 'Carmelite Friary Gatehouse, Burnham Norton: Scheduled Monument No. 21389: Excavations Prior to Installation of Staircase. 18 December 1995.' Unpublished report. Norfolk County Council, Norfolk Historic Environment Record, Source No. SNF93938

International Bee Research Association (IBRA), Bee Boles Register. https://www.beeboles.org.uk/en/bee-bole/0585 Accessed: 17 November 2020

National Heritage List for England (NHLE) official list entries. https://historicengland.org.uk

1013095 'St Mary's Carmelite Friary and Holy Well (1995)'. Accessed: 2000–21

1014862 'Binham Priory (1996)'. Accessed: 7 February 2022

1015271 'Creake Abbey (2013)'. Accessed: 15 July 2021

1015870 'Castle Acre Priory (1997)'. Accessed: 15 July 2021

1152454 'The Priory, Horsham St Faith and Newton St Faith (1984)'. Accessed: 15 July 2021

1220456 'Former Dominican Friary (Blackfriars) Norwich (2016)'. Accessed: 7 February 2022.

1342331 'Creake Abbey Farmhouse (1985)'. Accessed: 15 July 2021

1365164 'Church of St Mary, Sheepy Road [Atherstone] (1968)'. Accessed 16 February 2022

Norfolk Archaeological Trust, *Spring 2019 Newsletter*. https://www.
    norfarchtrust.org.uk/wp-content/uploads/2019/10/19.NATNewsletter
    2019web-v2.pdf
Norfolk Historic Environment Record (NHER) site summaries. https://
    www.heritage.norfolk.gov.uk Accessed: September 2020
    1377 'Post-medieval Malthouse [Brancaster]'
    1752 'Site of St Edmund's Church, Burnham Market'
    1753 'Site of St Andrew's Church, Burnham Market'
    1757 'Site of St Peter's Church, Burnham Thorpe'
    1774 'Site of Peterstone Priory'
    3977 'Site of Medieval Hospice, Swaffham'
    6690 'Mannington Hall'
Ordnance Survey 25 inch to the mile maps. https://maps.nls.uk/
Oxford Dictionary of Architecture (4th edn.) by James Stevens Curl and
    Susan Wilson. https://www.oxfordreference.com
Oxford Dictionary of National Biography (ODNB). https://www.oxforddnb.
    com
    'Brooke, George, ninth Baron Cobham (*c.*1497–1558)', by C.S. Knighton.
        Accessed: 8 January 2021
    'Cornwallis, Sir Charles (*c.*1555–1629)', by C.R. Kyle. Accessed:
        7 March 2019
    'Gresham, Sir Richard (*c.*1485–1549)', by I. Blanchard. Accessed:
        8 November 2018
    'Grimston Edward (1507/8–1600)', by C.S.L. Davies. Accessed:
        8 January 2021
    'Kerrich, Thomas (1748–1828)', by P. Tudor-Craig. Accessed:
        10 December 2019
    'Mary I (1516–1558)', by A. Weikel. Accessed: 8 November 2018
    'Radcliffe, Egremont (d. 1578)', by J. Lock. Accessed: 8 November 2018
    'Southwell, Sir Richard (1502/3–1564)', by S. Lehmberg. Accessed:
        7 March 2019
    'Warner, Sir Edward (1511–1565)', by C.P. Croly. Accessed:
        8 November 2018
UK Soil Observatory data. https://ukso.org Accessed: February 2021

Index

This index contains selected references. Page numbers in bold refer to illustrations and tables.

Printed in the United States
by Baker & Taylor Publisher Services